COBRA

WILLEMIJN STOKVIS

COBRA

An International Movement in Art after the Second World War

RIZZOLI
NEW YORK

© *1987 Ediciones Polígrafa, S. A.*

Translated from the Dutch by Jacob C. T. Voorthuis

First published in the United States
of America in 1988 by:

RIZZOLI INTERNATIONAL PUBLICATIONS, INC.
597 Fifth Avenue/New York 10017

Library of Congress Cataloging-in-Publication Data

Stokvis, Willemijn.
    Cobra: an international movement in art after
the Second World War.

    Translation of: Cobra.
    Bibliography: p.
    1. Cobra (Association).   2. Art, Modern—20th
century.   I. Title.
N6494.C5S8613   1988   709'.04   87-28604
ISBN 0-8478-0925-0

Printed in Spain by La Polígrafa, S. A.
Parets del Vallès (Barcelona)
Dep. Leg.: B. 38.595 - 1987

CONTENTS

The Cobra Movement

The Cobra, a deadly as well as a holy snake, was chosen, in the years immediately following the Second World War, as the symbol of a very lively international movement of Danish, Belgian and Dutch artists. In those chaotic times, when the damage of war was being surveyed and attempts were being made to start anew, the arts did not feature foremost in people's minds. Nevertheless, the devotion of the artists to their work was all the more vehement, and this was especially true of those who later became associated with Cobra.

Some of Cobra's members, such as the Danes Asger Jorn, Carl-Henning Pedersen, Henry Heerup and Egill Jacobsen, the Belgian Pierre Alechinsky and the Dutchmen Karel Appel, Constant and Corneille, were afterwards, during the fifties and sixties, to achieve considerable fame with their work. During and immediately after the war, however, they found it difficult to scrape together an existence. Even so, they were not solely concerned with expressing themselves creatively with the materials they could lay their hands on. With the movement they founded, they propounded their ideal of a new society. In this new world, which they felt to be close and of which they thought themselves to be pioneers, everyone would have not only the right to express himself creatively but the chance to do so as well.

The artists who came together in Cobra rejected rational Western culture, which, as could be seen from the Second World War, had shown itself to be rotten to the core. Wishing to reach the very source of human creativity, they took their examples from those forms of art which appeared not to have been tainted with the rules and conventions of the Western World: from, for example, primitive peoples with their totems and their magic signs, from Eastern calligraphy, from prehistoric art and from the art of the Middle Ages. They did find some unspoilt aspects of Western culture, such as the still thriving forms of folk art, naive art and the creative products of children and the mentally handicapped. Apart from these, handwriting was considered to be the most direct expression of one's personal psyche. The artists, in fact, were performing a conscious regression, a return to the archetypal images of fantasy thought to lie hidden under the many layers of the human subsconscious, an idea formulated by the Swiss psychologist Carl Gustav Jung, whom many of their generation read and admired.

Their appreciation of what was called primitive expression did not just stem from a search for truth, origins and real life far removed from the formalism of the Western World. They, and many others of their generation, were struck anew by the powerful expression of the irrational shapes and colours in primitive art, as had already happened in the early years of the century with the French Fauvists and Cubists as well as the German Expressionists. They hoped to preserve something of that beauty in their own work, even though it had been deemed unworthy and suppressed by the rules of schools and academies. In their search for it they experimented with paint, wood, clay, words and sounds, etc.

The Cobra movement, which was founded in November 1948 and survived until November 1951, can with some justification, and for the time being at least, be called the last great avant-garde movement of the century. The name is made up of the first letters of those of the cities where its members lived and worked: Copenhagen, Brussels and Amsterdam. Later movements, or even contemporary ones, do not seem to have had that revolutionary élan so characteristic of avant-garde movements. After 1945, indeed, it was more often than not the art critics, galleries or museums that grouped artists together in any particular category.

The underlying motive for Cobra's revolutionary activities was the Marxist philosophy which many of its artists adhered to, but propagated especially by the three leading members, the Danish artist-philosopher Asger Jorn, the Belgian poet, and later calligrapher, Christian Dotremont and the Dutch painter Constant Nieuwenhuys. Apart from any affinity they shared on artistic grounds, it was with this conviction particularly that they found themselves to have common interests. By analogy with the Communist International, in November 1949 they renamed their movement *The International of Experimental Artists.* The international fraternization and cooperation that existed for a short time within the movement is unique, and for this particular reason Cobra cannot be compared to any other avant-garde movement of this century.

Within Cobra, anti-aestheticism and anti-specialization were the order of the day. Painters wrote poetry, poets painted and drew, they established contacts with filmmakers, fashioned sculptures, took photographs, made works of art from rubbish, worked together on murals, canvas and paper. Although these artists vehemently rejected every kind of formalism or stylization, a definite Cobra "language" or style did evolve through their collaboration, at least in their paintings, which continued to develop even after 1951. In retrospect, it was this style or painterly language that gave the movement its prominent place in the history of modern art. With this language, Cobra attuned itself to the mood of abstract expressionism that was to dominate Western culture in the fifties, even though it appeared under different names. In America the artists that worked in this way were grouped under the name *Abstract Expressionism*, although for some of them the term *Action Painting* was used. In France it was called *Abstraction Lyrique* or *Tachisme*, though some artists, such as the Frenchman Jean Dubuffet, were grouped under the name *Informal Art*. Many artists who cannot be easily placed within a definite category come under this heading, which I would like to call the *second great wave of Primitive Expressionism* that emerged in the art of the twentieth century; the first, which had geared itself rather more to visible reality, had flourished especially in Germany, around 1910.

The Expressionism that surfaced everywhere during and immediately after the Second World War was founded on the basis of surrealistic movements and was, at the same time, a reaction against them. Surrealism had spread like an oil slick over the world of the thirties and had, with its search into the subsconscious, added an enormous arsenal of subjects to the artists' choice. Their search, however, had confined itself exclusively to the individual subconscious, from which these Surrealists, in the footsteps of Freud, evoked distressing visions of sexual dreams. The postwar generation had dug deeper and come up with the mythical and collective layers of that hidden world. These artists replaced automatism (the method used by Surrealists to evoke images from their subconscious) with spontaneity. They exchanged the stifling world of the Surrealist's imagination for a vibrant explosion of emotion in the colours, shapes and materials with which they worked. The "Primitive Expressionism" that came after 1945 found a theoretical stronghold in the Cobra movement, where the dependence upon Surrealism, and the break with it, were most successfully formulated.

The basis for the original contribution that Cobra made to this expressionism was established in Denmark before and during the war.

Preludes

DENMARK

In 1934, just after the Surrealist movement *Linien* (the Line) had been founded in Denmark, a split in this group was provoked by the painter and art theorist Ejler Bille, a split that was to be repeated on an international scale years later with the founding of Cobra in Paris in November 1948. By 1939 this split was to lead a group of artists in Denmark to evolve an uninhibited expressionist style. It was not in fact Bille who gave the starting signal for this new style, but Egill Jacobsen, who, during a stay in Paris in the winter of 1935-36, had been greatly influenced by Picasso and had started painting barbaric masks. Unlike the mask-like works of Picasso, however, these were not based on an analysis of the real thing but appeared more like new creatures, unexpectedly created from the imagination. Jacobsen wanted to equal what he called Picasso's "tangible brush technique" and "to paint more expressionistically than the German Expressionists themselves," whom he found "still too much tied down to a naturalist way of thinking."

The painting called *Obhobning* (Pile-up), which he had done towards the end of 1938 (Fig. 38), was found to be of great inspiration. In it he painted man, surrounded by darkness, dreaming of freedom and revolution. He later said he had painted it as a reaction to the German invasion of Czechoslovakia. He let the paint drip, spatter and run rampant, like the untamed forces that he wanted to visualize.

Curiously enough, all of this happened at about the same time that Jackson Pollock, on the other side of the ocean, was abandoning his realistic style and concentrating on the substance of paint.

The example set by Egill Jacobsen suddenly revealed the direction the artists around him should take. From 1939 onwards they evolved an art form through which in their own way they endeavoured to evoke archetypal images from their subconscious, in which they felt themselves to be closely related to the art of Scandinavian prehistory and the forms of folk art that were still practised here and there. They were also seriously interested in psychology and even let themselves be analysed by a psychiatrist who was, more or less, a member of the group.

These Danish artists, who called themselves *Mythologizing Artists* or *Experimentalists*, strove to clear the way, as Carl Henning Pedersen put it, for the urge present in all people to express themselves, an urge which was being suppressed by existing rules and conventions. The desire to create a new art for the people, by giving rein to the uninhibited expression of the people, was closely bound up with a Marxist vision of society. "We must make all the people artists, because they are artists. It is only that they don't think so themselves. They believe that art is something for which you have to study and that only very special people are able to learn it. They don't know that art is within everyone, and that it will only come to the surface by man trying to feel his way about, by his playing with stones, colours, words and sounds." Pedersen wrote this in 1944. The year before he had made a plea for the establishment of *Art Libraries* throughout the country. The state should take over the products of the artists, who in their turn would receive the necessities of life. The works of art, being the property of the state, could then be borrowed by everyone for their homes, "just as is the case with books at the moment."

Such ideas for a new society did not only have their origin in the Marxist convictions of these Danish artists. Much earlier, in the first half of the nineteenth century, such a concept had been proposed by the Danish clergyman-poet Nicolai Fred. Sev. Grundtvig (1783-1872). He had made an enormous effort to involve people, especially farmers, with culture and had laid the foundations for the Folk High Schools which subsequently spread throughout the country from the second half of the nineteenth century onwards, an example which was not followed in other countries until the twentieth century. Many of the artists who were to become involved with Cobra had, as was usual in Denmark, visited these Folk High Schools and were familiar with Grundtvig's ideas.

However, it wasn't only in their social ideas that they anticipated the Cobra movement. The works they produced from 1938 or 1939 onwards were later to be dubbed "Cobra work," presented at Cobra exhibitions and reproduced in the Cobra publications.

EGILL JACOBSEN (*b*. 1910) was only once to use his paint as freely as he had done in the painting called *Obhobning*. The rest of his work is made up of vividly coloured masks, creatures which are half animal and half vegetable, and some abstract compositions with rhythmically grouped lines and surfaces which he applied to the strains of jazz music (Figs. 39-42). In this work, which he has continued to produce to this day, he seems to have given a new lease of life to an old barbaric world of folklore.

EJLER BILLE (*b.* 1910) had been the first to rebel against orthodox Surrealism, urging his fellow artists not to give themselves over to dreams any longer, but to allow their creative imagination free rein. But it wasn't until Jacobsen gave his example that Bille knew which direction to take, even though his own sculptures (Fig. 43), which he had been making since 1931, did contain mysterious signs and masks, which he would sometimes colour brightly. In his painting he remained imprisoned in well-thought-out abstract compositions, with weak, Arp-like shapes and wavy lines. In 1938 his work exploded into vivid colours and wild patches (Figs. 44-46). Besides Jacobsen's work, that of the Spanish Surrealist painter Joan Miró, who was to have a profound influence on the whole Cobra movement, was of great importance to him. Around 1948-49, however, his thoughtful nature brought him back to the making of still compositions, using warm, subdued colours (Fig. 47).

CARL-HENNING PEDERSEN (*b.* 1913), who for a time had dabbled in geometric abstraction, began in 1937 to

EJLER BILLE: *Maske Fortegn* (Mask, Sign), 1936. Artificial stone, height 30 cm. Private collection, Denmark.

draw masks. Reacting very differently to Jacobsen's work, it suddenly became clear to him that his direction lay in fantasy, the world of fairy tales and mythology, and so children's drawings and certain forms of folk art became his sources of inspiration. From 1938-39 onwards, a mysterious world can be seen to emerge in his work, a world in which huge animals and gods make man appear a helpless creature. One is strongly reminded of the rough, direct style of painting used by the German Expressionists of *Die Brücke*, as also of the warm colours and poetical designs of Chagall. One cannot help thinking that paintings by artists like Carl-Henning Pedersen, and those of several of his friends, could only have been made in the country of that great fairy-tale writer, Hans Christian Andersen (Figs. 28-30).

During the war, Pedersen's world of fables was cloaked in darkness. The threatening deep blues, the sombre reds and greens, cleared after 1945, giving way to a very light palette, with lots of white and yellow characterizing his work from then on. The subjects he depicted were put down in large spots which had something sparkling, something festive, about them (Figs. 31-35). Pedersen, who also writes poetry, has said himself about this way of working: "I want to catch the golden sunlight and capture it on my canvas." Egill Jacobsen wrote of Pedersen's work in 1941: "Creative abstract art is not narrative, but a form of life in itself, much like what the fetish is for the negro, or what poetry, music and fables are for our culture.... The imagination will make its prison explode. Fantasy and reality will become as one, as they already are in fairy tales, in poetry and in the paintings of Carl-Henning Pedersen."

The painter ELSE ALFELT (1910-1974), Pedersen's wife, moved from geometric abstraction, which had been characteristic of her work until 1941, to a form of landscape painting in which she developed an abstract motif of high, rocky peaks with a piercing sun. This motif continued to fascinate her throughout her later development, becoming increasingly charming and poetical in expression (Fig. 58). In 1945 she allowed herself a momentary diversion with a freer play of colours and brushstrokes, clearly inspired by Kandinsky (Fig. 59).

The sculptor-painter HENRY HEERUP (*b.* 1907) also belonged to their circle. He seemed for some reason to embody all that the others so much desired to become,

CARL-HENNING PEDERSEN: Title page and two subsequent pages from his anthology of poetry entitled *Drömmedigte* (Dream poems), illustrated by Pedersen himself and published in Copenhagen in 1945 as a "Helhesten publication."

namely a real folk artist. As long ago as the early thirties, Henry Heerup started making very original works of stone, wood or other *objets trouvés* in his workshop, which was just a shed in a field somewhere outside Copenhagen. He let himself be guided completely by the material, which, "if it demanded it," he painted. Of his favourite material, granite, he said: "There's always something within the stone itself. Granite is the hard-boiled egg of nature." He wanted to free the shapes that he felt were hidden in this "hard-boiled egg," or indeed in any other material he could lay his hands on (Figs. 48, 51 & 57).

The constantly recurring archetypal symbols for love, fertility and death in his sculptures and paintings remind one of folk art, though his style does show strong links with the melancholy Scandinavian expressionism (Figs. 49, 55 & 56). Humour also plays an important part in Heerup's work, particularly in his junk-sculptures (Figs. 50, 52, 53 & 54). He himself names Picasso as his greatest source of inspiration; probably, however, he also saw reproductions of Dadaist and Surrealist objects. For variety Heerup was always busy composing songs which he would play on his recorder. He wrote down the music in a songbook which was illustrated by his own hand. The shed in the field, where he often shelters from bad weather, is covered with mysterious signs, possibly to frighten away any evil spirits that might disturb his concentration.

The youngest of the group, Asger Jörgensen, was to play a leading role. From 1945 onwards, he called himself simply ASGER JORN (1914-1973). These artists infiltrated the exhibiting society *Höst* (Harvest) to such an extent that their predominance in it by 1942 earned them the name *Höstgroup*. In the meantime, Jorn had taken the initiative, in 1941, of starting the publication of a review. In it the artists expressed all their ideas. This review was called *Helhesten* (Horse of Hell), after an animal in Scandinavian mythology which has three legs and is the harbinger of death. The name was intended as an allusion to the Germans. As this Horse of Hell is in fact a sad creature, who wanders about neighing pathetically, unable to find any food for itself, they also found it an apt symbol of their own situation. Between 1941 and 1944, the review appeared some twelve times in all. It was illustrated with lithographs of their own making and in it they discussed such things as prehistory, forms of folk art, the frescoes adorning the medieval parish churches of Jutland,

primitive art, children's drawings and the work of their beloved Paul Klee. They also found room for things like psychology, jazz and cinema, in which they were profoundly interested.

Helhesten, which was later to serve as a model for the review of the Cobra movement, was not the only outlet for the ideas of the fiercely committed Jorn. Several other Danish reviews and papers carried articles from his pen during this period, among them the architectural review *A5* and the *Arbejderbladet* (Labour Review).

Jorn experienced great difficulty in attaining a freer way of expressing himself visually; in the end he found inspiration in the spontaneous style of Egill Jacobsen. The lessons he had had with Fernand Leger in Paris in 1936 and 1937 had disciplined him so rigorously that, as he himself wrote, it took him ten years to free himself completely from their influence. Only in a few of his prewar works — for example, in the barbaric painting called *Pige* (Girl), done in 1939 (Fig. 12) — does he appear to have found some of the freedom he sought, which did not really break through in his work until 1945. It must have been largely the irrational world of Klee and Miró that enabled Jorn to find his own style. His personal language becomes apparent in the series of etchings that he called *Occupations* and the series of watercolours which he painted during the war entitled *Didascale*, a combination of the name Dida, that of his loved one, and Asger, his own. From 1945 onwards he worked up the courage to express himself impetuously. With a long, never-ending line, winding its way through lots of small, brightly coloured patches, Jorn created a mysterious vegetative world in those years immediately following the war, a world in which countless tiny mythical creatures take shelter (Figs. 13-15).

There were other active participants in the *Höstgroup* and the circle around *Helhesten*, among them the painter Richard Mortensen and the sculptor Robert Jacobsen, who during the war fitted in completely with this mythologizing art. After the war, however, Mortensen and Jacobsen deliberately opted for geometric abstraction, thus taking a road in the opposite direction to the one followed by their former comrades and Cobra.

During the war they met regularly at Elise Johansen's house in the old centre of Copenhagen. Here they saw

A partition enclosing the choir stalls in the 12th-century Öjekapel, Dalarna, Sweden.

The shed in the grounds at Rodovre, near Copenhagen, where Heerup has worked for many years, and is still working (photographed in 1962).

Cover page of the first issue of the review *Helhesten* (Horse of Hell), published by the Danish experimentalists from March 1941 to November 1944. Cover by Henry Heerup.

themselves as a nucleus of resistance, with their *degenerate art*.

There were others in this group, such as the Icelandic painter SVAVAR GUDNASON (*b.* 1909), who had joined in 1940. In the following year he developed a dynamic abstract style dominated by cold colours (Fig. 66). The much younger painter ERIK ORTVAD (*b.* 1917) had joined the group earlier. Around 1941 or 1942 he developed a strange vegetative abstraction in his work, which some-times seemed to turn into vague creatures and which had a mysterious surreal feeling about it (Fig. 64). The sculptors ERIC THOMMESEN (*b.* 1916) and SONJA FERLOV (*b.* 1911) were also considered members of the group. They, however, were searching for extremely pure and concentrated forms, which they were to achieve, the one in wood and the other in plaster (sometimes cast in bronze), using a very laborious work-process (Figs. 60, 61, 62 & 63). Besides these, the poet Jörgen Nash (Asger Jorn's brother), the art critic Ole Sarving, the archaelogist P.V. Glob, the psychiatrist Sigurd Naesgaard, the architect Robert Dahlman Olsen and the well-known Danish writer Jens August Schade, all felt themselves to be closely asso-ciated with the group. They all contributed in some way, mostly in the form of articles for *Helhesten*. Various collections of poems, such as those of Nash, were provided with illustrations, anticipating a form of collaboration which was later to become so characteristic of Cobra.

Long before Cobra, Jorn was given the opportunity of putting his ideas about the integration of architecture and painting into practice. In 1943 he was asked to paint the walls of a country cottage belonging to the collector Elna Fonnesbech-Sandberg. Henry Heerup and Robert Jacobsen adorned the house with sculptures, and it was eventually described by a Danish magazine as "the abstract pancake house."

After the liberation, only Jorn felt the urge to expand his activities abroad and make contact with artists from other countries. There was in fact no immediate need for these artists to direct their attention away from Denmark. They were recognized in their own country and had enough opportunities of exhibiting their work in galleries, museums and exhibitions travelling throughout Scandi-navia. In 1948, four of them were chosen to represent Denmark at the Venice Biennale, which was something that Heerup had already done in 1936.

Meeting of the Revolutionary Surrealist Movement held in Brussels on 28th October 1947. From left to right: Max Bucaille, Christian Dotremont, Noël Arnaud, Joseph Istler and Asger Jorn.

Meanwhile, Jorn was going around with plans for the founding of an international review. Early in 1946 he travelled to Paris. There, in the studio of the hospi-table Jean-Michel Atlan, who was later to join Cobra, he met the poet and art promoter Edouard Jaguer and the writer Noel Arnaud, who were both to play important roles in the genesis of Cobra. In the autumn of the same year he met the Dutch painter Constant Nieuwenhuys at Pierre Loeb's gallery. Constant had been looking at Pierre's stock of Miró's work and he exchanged ideas with Jorn, who in turn showed him some work by the Danish group which he had brought with him. In the winter of 1946-47, Jorn wrote to Constant from Paris about the plans he had worked out for an international review which was to be called "Sarcoma." It took another two years for these plans to crystallize, though under the name of Cobra.

BELGIUM

Those in Belgium who were to devote themselves to Cobra were the younger followers of an important Surrealist movement that had existed in that country since 1925. The poet CHRISTIAN DOTREMONT(1922-1979), who was later to play a central role in the Cobra movement, had, after coming into contact with Surrealism in 1940, endeavoured to maintain and strengthen the existing contacts with the French representatives of that movement during the war. A rift had developed during this time between the Surreal-ists in Europe and their great leader André Breton, who had left for America. Disappointed by Breton's dismissive attitude to their political commitment on his return to Europe, Dotremont took the initiative of starting a new Surrealist movement, which he called *Le surréalisme révo-lutionnaire*. Dotremont himself led the Belgian branch of this movement, while the French poet Noel Arnaud organ-ized its French counterpart. Through their contacts with the Communist parties, which organized resistance activ-ities all over Europe, they arrived at a fierce combination of Surrealism and Communism, a combination which, as regards its direct practicality, Breton had discarded back in the early thirties. Many of these French and Belgian Surrealists (and many others besides) were ignorant of what was happening in Russia at the time and were ardent Stalinists!

The founding of Cobra, in Paris on 8th November 1948, was a direct result of conflict between the French and Belgian branches of this postwar movement. Even so, in the summer of 1948 they had been able to cooperate with each other on the publication of the only issue of a planned bimonthly review which had been christened *Le Surréalisme Révolutionnaire*. The Belgian revolutionary Surrealists, under the leadership of Christian Dotremont, had wanted to continue the combination of politics and art with vigour. The French, however, had already lost all faith in that combination and their branch was dissolved early in 1948. In November of that year, *Le Surréalisme Révolutionnaire* organized a conference in Paris at which the Belgians were able to manifest their enthusiasm for the convictions they held. The conference was attended by several avant-garde groups from different countries, who were to deliberate on "how to further organize the avant-garde"! The Belgians were supported by Asger Jorn, who acted as a representative for the Danish experimentalists, and who had been put in touch with this Belgian-French movement through Noel Arnaud. They were also given approval from the *Experimental Group in Holland*, which had been formed in the meantime, and which was represented by Constant, Appel and Corneille.

The political fervour of the Danes and the Dutch was slight in comparison with that of the Belgians. It did not, as with the Belgians and a few Danes, automatically involve membership of the Communist Party. Nevertheless, their shared Marxist convictions were probably the most important area of common ground. Marxism as adapted to the field of art was the basis for Cobra, which for them meant a complete integration of art with life. They did not want endless deliberation about theory and aesthetics, they wanted art to be absorbed into the normal process of living.

Strangely enough, it was this that separated them from the former French revolutionary Surrealists, who in 1947 had become exceedingly interested in a new stylistic development that was taking place in Paris at the time, the so-called *Abstraction Lyrique*. In retrospect, this style was comparable to the style that Cobra was to develop. It is hardly surprising, therefore, that two artists from the French corner, Jean-Michel Atlan and Jacques Doucet, were quick to join Cobra, and that the French art critics Michel Ragon and Edouard Jaguer were soon persuaded to lend their support and contribute to the Cobra movement.

The Belgian revolutionary Surrealists, however, were Surrealists of the old school. This gave Cobra a slightly unbalanced basis, as is clearly visible in the issues of the review *Cobra*, which was started early in 1949. The driving force behind Cobra in Belgium, and its international organizer, was Christian Dotremont. The Belgian supporting ranks were mainly composed of somewhat older Surrealist writers. Their contributions to the review and the reproductions of work by Belgian artists who had little or no connection with Cobra, but who in fact worked in the style of "Jeune Peinture Belge," which in turn was based on the "École de Paris," gave some issues of the review a rather chaotic character. Dotremont was conscious of this situation. Immediately before the founding of Cobra, he had written to Constant about the low level of his Belgian group as far as painting was concerned and how he planned to revive it by opening their eyes to the work of the Dutch and Danish experimentalist artists.

Appel, Corneille and Constant with a painted sculpture in wood by Appel, in Appel's studio, Oude Zijds, Voorburgwal, Amsterdam, 1948.

THE NETHERLANDS

The attitude to creative expression developed by the Danish spontaneous artists some years before the war had an immediate appeal for the young Dutch painters. Since their coincidental meeting in Paris a close relationship had developed between Jorn and Constant. People in the Netherlands were hardly aware of the existence of such a thing as Surrealism. Just a few artists had become familiar with its visual language through reproductions of paintings like those of Dalí and had ventured on the same path. The ideological theories of the movement, based on psychology, were not only unknown, but when the opportunity arose for people to become familiar with them, were to find very little sympathy. What did appeal directly to this country of painters was the expressionist handling of Surrealism in the work and ideas of the Danish Experimentalists.

CONSTANT (Constant Anton Nieuwenhuys, *b.* 1920), with Jorn's encouragement, became the driving force behind the organization of the *Experimental Group in Holland.* Together with KAREL APPEL (*b.* 1921) and CORNEILLE (Corneille Guillaume Beverloo, *b.* 1922), he made up the active nucleus of the group. Determined to find their own direction, they had been experimenting since 1946.

Most of the Dutch artists who were to join Cobra were some ten years younger than their Danish counterparts and had not had the chance to acquaint themselves with the latest developments in art. The Netherlands were not only ignorant of the existence of Surrealism, for Dadaism had also gone unnoticed. Even the important Dutch avant-garde group De Stijl had only found a response among a small circle of people. The Netherlands had retreated into provincial isolation, where only traditional values could prevail, and the German occupation had made this isolation complete. During the war, cultural life had been squeezed into the straitjacket of the all-controlling *Kultuur Kamer* (House of Culture), which had been set up in the Netherlands especially, parallel to the German *Kultur-kammer*, as the Netherlands had traditionally been considered part of the *Great German Reich*. Those who adamantly refused to join the Kultuur Kamer could neither exhibit their work nor buy any materials. The strangling controls made effective by the occupying forces led to an almost total stagnation of cultural life.

With the opening of the borders in 1945, many went off to see what was happening elsewhere in order to cast off the oppressive seclusión which the war had forced upon them. Appel and Corneille, who had known each other from their time at the academy in the early days of the war, came into contact with Belgian painters from Jeune Peinture Belge in 1946 and through them learned of the newest developments in the École de Paris. They were particularly taken with the work of the young French painter Edouard Pignon. While still enthusiastically digesting these influences, they were confronted in 1947 with the work of Joan Miró, Paul Klee and Jean Dubuffet, who were to lead them in a completely different direction. When in Paris, which was then still the Mecca of modern art, and where Constant had been before them in 1946, they came into contact with the as yet barely recognized vanguard of the arts. Several of those who were later to join the Experimental Group in Holland at that time studied the many forms of primitive art which could be seen in Paris at the Musée de l'Homme.

In the Netherlands, Willem Sandberg, who had been appointed director of Amsterdam's Stedelijk Museum in

1945, tried to break through his country's formal artistic climate with exhibitions of work by Picasso, Matisse, Braque and Paul Klee. In the meantime he was constantly searching for new talent, and as early as 1946 or 1947 his eye had fallen on some of the artists who were later to be united under the Cobra flag.

Appel, Constant and Corneille underwent all sorts of influences in quick succession. The decorative cubism of the École de Paris turned out to have little to offer them. They wanted to find an outlet for their strong inner drive, feeling themselves to be more closely related to their own fellow countryman Vincent van Gogh and the German Expressionists. Apart from those, they greatly admired Picasso. They were quick to discover that the creative work of primitive peoples, children and the mentally handicapped could show them their direction.

After his meeting with Jorn in 1946, grim creatures of the imagination started appearing in Constant's work (Fig. 80), but that of Appel and Corneille did not begin to show an individual primitivist form of expression until the winter of 1947-48. The moment that breakthrough occurred in Appel's work, he wrote enthusiastically to Corneille: "Corneille, just a quick note. I'm working day and night, now I've started painting. Suddenly I discovered it (at night). I've started powerful primitive work, more powerful than Negro art and Picasso. Why? Because I continue in the twentieth century, spring from Picasso. Bright colours. I have broken through the wall of abstraction, Surrealism, etc. My work contains everything; you mustn't get stuck in a groove. Don't come for the time being, no time. Work hard, throw everything overboard. Your friend, Karel." Whereas Appel started creating barbaric and childish imaginary beings in his collages, gouaches and paintings, which have become so characteristic of the period when he was finding his own style (Fig. 67), Corneille for his part abandoned himself during the same period to a wild play of shapes and colours that are strongly reminiscent of the work of Miró (Fig. 91).

Of the other artists who joined them later, THEO WOLVECAMP (b. 1925) had, in 1947, started working in a very free abstract style, sometimes using sand on his canvases. Apart from Miró, Kandinsky's abstract expressionist period was an important source of inspiration for him (Figs. 106 & 108). ANTON ROOSKENS (1906-1976),

being a lot older than the others, had already been through a whole career as a painter before being brought into contact with them; nevertheless, he belonged to those who wanted to go in a different direction after the war. He rejected his expressionist style, which was reminiscent of Van Gogh and the Flemish painter Permeke, absorbing the influence of Picasso and Matisse quickly in order to give himself up to the idiom of primitive art (Figs. 102 & 103). Of this art he, like so many others among the experimentalists, started a collection. JAN NIEUWENHUYS (1922-1986), Constant's brother, was a member for only a short time. After undergoing the influence of the École de Paris, he started using fish and imaginary creatures to make compositions of a strange, surreal character (Fig. 107). Apart from these, he also produced totem-like objects. EUGÈNE BRANDS (b. 1913), who, like Rooskens, was older than the others, went through a completely individual development as a self-taught artist. Around 1939 or 1940 he started making surreal compositions of *objets trouvés*, and during the war he began to experiment with blotting, smudging and spattering with ink and watercolours. He was searching for the magical element in everything. This brought him to the art of primitive peoples, whose music and ritual objects he began to collect at an early stage.

The *Experimental Group in Holland* was founded at Constant's house on 16th July 1948. Brands hesitated and joined a little later. In the autumn of 1948 three poets joined the group: JAN GOMMERT ELBURG (b. 1919), GERRIT KOUWENAAR (b. 1923) and LUCEBERT (the pseudonym of Lubertus Jacobus Swaanswijk, b. 1924). The last-named was also soon to become an important painter and draughtsman. It was a phenomenon peculiar to the Netherlands that a movement called "experimental poetry" grew up, parallel to "experimental visual art."

During the group's first meeting they decided to look for contacts with similar groups at home and abroad and to start the publication of a review that would propagate the group's ideas. The plans for this review, which was to be called *Reflex*, were quick to materialize. The first issue, which appeared between September and October of 1948, was completely taken up by a militant manifesto written by Constant. In this manifesto, which he had written some time before the founding of Cobra, he

The Dutch Experimental Group in Appel's studio, autumn 1948. From left to right: (above) Appel, Elburg, Kouwenaar; (below) Wolvecamp, Corneille, Constant, Jan Nieuwenhuys, Brands and Rooskens. (Lucebert was not present.)

Reflex, review of the *Experimental Group in Holland*, No. 1, September/October 1948, with cover by Corneille.

summed up in clear language what that movement was to be about. Although he himself had been occupied with Marxism during the war, there can be little doubt that it was his contact with Jorn that formed the basis for what he wrote in this manifesto. His heated arguments are especially valid for the international situation. When, for example, he directs his guns against Surrealism, his attack begins to sound rather like a tilting with windmills; or so at least it must have sounded to the Dutch, who had remained almost untouched by that movement. Constant was not supported in his theories, and he was the only one to sign the manifesto. The other members of the Dutch group preferred to occupy themselves with the practice of art.

The Movement

When these Danes, Belgians and Dutchmen assembled to found Cobra, on 8th November 1948 at the Café Notre Dame in Paris, they had behind them very different backgrounds. Apart from the similarity of outlook they could discern in each other, the most striking feature characterizing the group was their enthusiasm for working together. They did this, not just by publishing the review *Cobra*, or by organizing exhibitions, but also by collaborating with great fervour on works of art.

THE PUBLICATIONS

The plans so long cherished by Jorn for an international publication finally crystallized in the review *Cobra*. It was to be the pivot of the whole movement. When publication ceased, in November 1951, it became obvious that the movement had come to an end. Dotremont, who had been elected general secretary of the group, also became editor in chief of the review. In concept it could be compared to *Helhesten*, reflecting the many-sided and somewhat chaotic character of the Cobra movement. Eight issues appeared in all; it would have been eleven, but for the fact that the Danish double issue (Nos. 8 & 9) and the Swedish issue had been stopped at the preparatory stage. The contents range from manifestoes written by members of the group to observations, comments and reports. The review contained prose, poetry and articles on such varied subjects as writing, folk art, cinema and the work of artists that interested the members of Cobra. In addition there were contributions largely by Belgian writers and filmmakers with whom the group felt some affinity. The review, which was lavishly illustrated with reproductions

Cobra party, Denmark, November 1948. From the left, around the table: Constant, Christian Dotremont, Eljer Bille, Ragna Ortvad (under the lamp), Henry Heerup (half-hidden), Erik Ortvad, Carl-Henning Pedersen, Tony Appel and, in the foreground, Corneille.

Christian Dotremont, general secretary of the Cobra movement and editor in chief of the review *Cobra*, sitting at his typewriter, Brussels, 1950. (On the wall to the right a painted relief in wood by Constant.)

Front and back covers of *Cobra*, No. 1, published in Copenhagen in 1949. Lithograph by Asger Jorn, Carl-Henning Pedersen and Egill Jacobsen, 31 × 49 cm, signed on reverse, above left and right and below right.

Front and back covers of *Cobra*, No. 3, published in Brussels in June 1949. Lithograph by Pierre Alechinsky, 27.5 × 44 cm, signed below right.

of paintings and sculptures, also contained, as had been the case with *Helhesten* and *Reflex*, a number of original lithographs done by members of Cobra. Most of the issues published (five out of a possible eight) came out in Brussels. The first number was produced and published in Copenhagen, the fourth in Amsterdam and the fifth in Hanover. This last was put together by the editor of the German avant-garde review *Meta*, the painter Karl Otto Götz, who had come into contact with Cobra in 1949. In the first issue, which appeared in March 1949, Jorn published an article in which he formulated Cobra's position in relation to Surrealism. He took the first, and most widely-known, definition of Surrealism (by Breton), and applied it to the convictions of the experimentalist artists. Jorn put experiment and spontaneity in the place of *psychic automatism*; he did not share Breton's wish to let dreams dominate one's whole life. Jorn's definition of the experimentalists' ideas is as follows: "Our experimenting is geared to the uninhibited expression of thought beyond the control of reason. Through this irrational spontaneity we have reached the vital source of being. Our aim is to escape the tyranny of reason so as eventually to establish the sovereignty of life."

The Cobra group also published an information bulletin called *Le Petit Cobra*, of which four numbers appeared in all. It gave reports about events in the group and information concerning the activities of its individual members. Details were also given about other avant-garde groups which had sprung up after the war, in or even outside Europe. Lastly, one of the few young Belgian Surrealist writers involved with Cobra, the poet Joseph Noiret (*b.* 1927), produced a number of *Tout Petits Cobras*. Each of these consisted of a single sheet of paper, with a poem by himself or a text by some well-known writer or painter which was relevant to Cobra. Numerous "Cobra publications" appeared in Copenhagen, Brussels and Amsterdam, in the form of little booklets. In 1950, for instance, Jorn produced the first fifteen volumes of what was called the *Bibliothèque de Cobra* (the plans for a further series never materialized), in which the work of an equal number of painters and sculptors was reproduced and discussed in a short accompanying text. In Holland, too, a number of booklets appeared as "Cobra publications," in which painters and poets worked together, placing text and illustration side by side as elements of equal value or making them interweave in a single whole (Fig. 6). The Belgian "Cobra publications" consisted of literary and theoretical texts in which the illustration, though present, played a subordinate role.

EXHIBITIONS

The series of larger or smaller exhibitions held individually or collectively by the different groups taking part in Cobra, together with their various publications, form the "public" history of the movement.

The series began in Copenhagen during the months of November and December 1948, with a *Höst* exhibition

Eight of the fifteen volumes comprised in the first series of the *Bibliothèque de Cobra*, published in Copenhagen in 1950 under the name "Artistes libres" (in French and Danish). From left to right: (above) No. 1, Pierre Alechinsky (text by Luc Zangrie); No. 3, Karel Appel (text by Edouard Jaguer); No. 4, Jean-Michel Atlan (text by Michel Ragon); No. 6, Constant (text by Christian Dotremont); (below) No. 7, Corneille (text by Christian Dotremont); No 12, Henry Heerup (text by Christian Dotremont); No. 14, Asger Jorn (text by Christian Dotremont); No. 15, Carl-Henning Pedersen (text by Christian Dotremont).

in which the whole Dutch experimental group had been invited to take part. Appel, Constant and Corneille had travelled to Denmark and were warmly received. The confrontation with work of the Danish experimentalists proved a revelation to them. "Life contains emotions which will stay with you forever, and the first look at those pictures was just such a revelation," was what Corneille wrote in his report on the journey, which was published in the second (and last) issue of their review *Reflex*. The work that made the deepest impression on them, apart from that of Jorn and Egill Jacobsen, was that of Carl-Henning Pedersen, which by then had matured considerably.

During March 1949, the Belgians held an international Cobra exhibition in Brussels which was called *La Fin et Les Moyens* (The End and the Means). Work was exhibited by members from the three Cobra countries, as well as by artists from elsewhere who had joined the movement. In the list of people taking part in this exhibition, published in the catalogue which served simultaneously as the second issue of the review *Cobra*, one comes across names like that of the painter (later a sculptor) Pol Bury, who only fleetingly took part in Cobra. It was an important event for the Belgian group, however, for it

marked the moment when the young painter and graphic artist Pierre Alechinsky (*b*. 1927) was brought into contact with the movement through a visit to the exhibition; he was later to become one of its most active members.

After this relatively small international exhibition, two larger ones were to take place, the first of which was held at Amsterdam's Stedelijk Museum from the 3rd to the 28th of November 1949. It was to be the highlight of the movement's short history. Artists from ten different countries, many of whom attended the official opening, took part in this exhibition, which had been designed in a revolutionary way by the Dutch architect Aldo van Eyck. Appel, Constant and Brands had completed three enormous canvases just a few days before the exhibition opened, and these — together with a painting by Corneille in the form of a cube — were placed at strategic points in the exhibition rooms. The visitors were shouted at by aggressive figures, shaking their fists, in the painting by Constant which had been placed at the entrance. After that the visitor was guided through a wooden cage, painted black, to which the works of the Dutch experimentalist poets were attached.

a

d

b

e

c

f

(a) The Experimentalists taking their work to the Stedelijk Museum in Amsterdam for the important Cobra exhibition held in November 1949. From left to right: Rooskens, a passer-by, Schierbeek (with a painting by Gilbert), Wolvecamp, Brands, Götz, Corneille, Doucet, Alechinsky, Tony Appel, Lucebert, Elburg, Tajiri, Kouwenaar, Constant, Appel, Victor Nieuwenhuys (with a painting by his father, Constant).

(b) International exhibition of "Cobra" experimental art at the Stedelijk Museum, Amsterdam, 3-28 November 1949. The broad corridor at the entrance to the exhibition. On the wall in the background, *Barricade*, the picture specially painted for the exhibition by Constant.

(c) Tony Appel and Aldo van Eyck hanging a room with work by Appel in the Stedelijk Museum, Amsterdam, November 1949. (Van Eyck is carrying a painting by Constant entitled *The Witch's Beast*.)

(d, e, f) The three photographs on the left were taken in Amsterdam in November 1949, the two at the top in Constant's house, the third during the party after the opening of the exhibition. Those present include: Appel, Corneille, Constant, Tony Appel, Else Alfelt, Tajiri, Doucet, Aldo van Eyck, Henny Riemens, Carl-Henning Pedersen, Erik Ortvad and K.O. Götz.

16

The core of the exhibition was made up by the Danish and Dutch experimentalist groups, which were represented almost in their entirety. The only Belgian participant, however, was Alechinsky. Karl Otto Götz had provided contributions from six modern German painters, counting himself. Stephen Gilbert and his friend William Gear represented England; they had made contact with the group in Paris. Jacques Doucet and Jean-Michel Atlan came from France and, from Czechoslovaquia, Joseph Istler, who, together with the French painters, had already been involved with the Revolutionary Surrealists. America was represented by the sculptor Shinkichi Tajiri, who felt increasingly bound up with the Dutch. Österlin came from Sweden; he was one of the three members of the group called *Imaginisterna* (The Imaginists), with which Cobra maintained contacts. From Switzerland, finally, came the painter-sculptor Zoltan Kemeny (*d*. 1965) and his wife Madeleine, with whom Corneille had got in touch in the course of his enormous correspondence.

The fourth issue of the review *Cobra* served as the catalogue to the exhibition. On its cover it had a large open mouth with an enormous tongue sticking out at the public. This exhibition caused quite a stir among the Dutch. The papers were filled with news of the show, though they had little praise for it. On a Saturday, two days after the opening in the Stedelijk Museum, a riot took place which the papers blew up into a major scandal, but which only resulted in the exhibition attracting still greater numbers of visitors. The group had planned to hold a reading of experimental literature that evening, enlivened by authentic folk music. Dotremont began the evening by reading from the second part of his lengthy battle cry and manifesto *Le grand rendez-vous naturel* (The great natural gathering), the first part of which had appeared as an introduction to the exhibition and an appendix to *Cobra* No. 4. The fact that the reading was in French, and that most of those present did not understand that language but did grasp the meaning of the word *Soviétique*, which occurred repeatedly in Dotremont's text, caused the room to become rowdy and fighting to break out. In the end the premises had to be cleared by the police. The storm that broke loose in the press was answered by Dotremont in a pamphlet entitled *Je ne vais dans les musées que pour enlever les muselières* (I only enter museums to remove gags), in which he refuted everything the papers had written.

The Dutch experimental poets, as seen through the bars of the cage in which they were hanging, at the November 1949 exhibition in Amsterdam: (below) Kouwenaar (middle, from left to right) Bert Schierbeek, Lucebert and Elburg; (above) the German painter K.O. Götz.

Cartoon entitled *After the Experiment*, published in "Het Parool" (end of November beginning of December 1949). It shows Sandberg sweeping the floor after the Cobra exhibition in his museum.

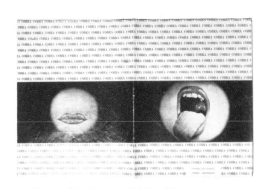

Front and back covers of *Cobra*, No. 4, published in Amsterdam in November 1949. Photomontage by the Danish film-maker Jörgen Roos and the Danish Surrealist painter Wilhelm Freddie, 30.6 × 48.3 cm.

Cover of *Cobra*, No. 7, published in Brussels in the autumn of 1950, with a reproduction of a slate engraving by Raoul Ubac.

Babylonian representation of the symbol of heaven: a snake coiled in spirals. This appeared in many Cobra publications as an emblem of the movement.

Symbol of a snake on one of two 4th-century gold horns, found near Gallehus (Denmark) in the 17th and 18th centuries respectively, also used as an emblem of the movement in many Cobra publications.

This eventful evening caused a rift to appear in the *Experimental Group in Holland*, resulting in the departure of the painters Rooskens, Brands and Wolvekamp (the last-named soon changed his mind), and the poets Elburg, Lucebert and Kouwenaar, as well as Bert Schierbeek, who had joined the group shortly before the exhibition.

The next day an International Cobra Congress was held, at which it was decided to expand the Danish-Belgian-Dutch "Cobra front" and to call the movement *Internationale des Artistes Expérimentaux* (I.A.E.) as well as simply Cobra, whereby the entry of artists of whatever nationality in the movement was officially recognized.

The second great international Cobra exhibition was held at the Palais des Beaux-Arts in Liège from 6th October to 6th November 1951. This exhibition was organized by Alechinsky — with the help of the Danish writer Uffe Harder, who by that time had joined the Danish experimentalists — and was again designed by the architect Aldo van Eyck. This exhibition signalled the end of the movement. Jorn had been admitted to the Silkeborg sanatorium in the summer of 1951. In November of that year Dotremont was admitted to the same institution. He was later to write: "Is it just because of Jorn's illness and mine that we write the words 'The End' on the tenth issue of our review? Doubtless we wanted to stop the business at once rather than wait for some explosion in the future. 'Mourir en Beauté' is our last slogan. The only true deliberation in Cobra is its end."

The plan, for which the museum in Liège provided financial help, was to make the exhibition even larger than the one in Amsterdam. It showed not only the work of the movement's members but also, by way of homage, a few examples of work by internationally known artists such as Joan Miró, Alberto Giacometti, Wifredo Lam and Jean Bazaine. There were also works by Belgian artists who were in some way connected with Cobra, such as the painters Jan Cox, Louis van Lint, Georges Collignon (the leader of a group which called itself *Cobra Réalité*, but which was completely independent of Cobra and had in fact very little in common with it) and Raoul Ubac, who had emigrated to France before the war and did Surrealist photographs and engravings on slate. With all these new elements the exhibition, for which the tenth issue of *Cobra* served as a catalogue, was given a different and more official character than the one held at the Stedelijk Museum in Amsterdam.

The *Deuxième Exposition Internationale d'Art Expérimental* in Liège was held to coincide with the *Petit Festival du Film Expérimental et Abstrait*, which was organized by the film-maker, and later painter, Jean Raine. The Belgian group had always shown a great interest in several avant-garde film-makers. When the *Festival Mondial du Film et des Beaux-Arts de Belgique* was being held at Knokke-Le-Zoute in June and July 1949, these film-makers had been allowed to fill almost the whole of the third issue of the review with their articles.

In 1950 the film-maker Luc de Heusch (using the pseudonym Luc Zangrie), who, like Raine, was in close contact with Cobra, worked with Raine on a Cobra film. It was called *Persephone* and was based on a little book written by Alechinsky entitled *Les Poupées de Dixmude*, which had been published by Cobra. The *Petit Festival* in Liège gave a survey of the history of experimental and abstract cinema.

Apart from these three international exhibitions, there were numerous smaller exhibitions held in the countries directly involved with Cobra. Several of these had an international character in the sense that foreign guest artists participated in them. We find examples of this in Denmark with the exhibitions of the *Höst* society in 1948 and 1949, and those of the group called *Spiralen* (The Spiral), which Jorn had joined in 1949 when the *Höst* group was dissolved. To mark the publication of the sixth issue of *Cobra* an exhibition was held at the Galerie Apollo in Brussels. The painters represented were Corneille, Österlin, Götz, Jorn and the Flemish painter-writer Hugo Claus, who was later to be involved in several Cobra activities, though his main commitment was to the Dutch experimentalist poets. Some of the exhibitions organized by the Belgians and held in Brussels, such as *L'objet à travers les âges* (The object through the ages) in August 1949 and *Les développements de l'œil, exposition de photographie de Daguerre à Ubac* (The development of the eye, an exhibition of photography from Daguerre to Ubac) in the autumn of 1950, though bearing the name of Cobra, confirmed the extent to which the Belgians were rooted in orthodox Surrealism.

Some members succeeded in having exhibitions of their work in Paris during the Cobra years. A few of the Dutch experimental painters were able to show their work at Colette Alendy's small gallery, both in 1950 and in 1951. In February 1951 a reasonably extensive Cobra exhibition was held at the *Librairie 73 boulevard St. Michel*, where art works as well as several documents relating to Cobra were shown. This exhibition was organized by the writer and art critic Michel Ragon. Also in 1951, there was an exhibition at the Galerie Pierre of work by *5 peintres de Cobra*, among the five being the painter Mogens Balle, who, coming from the Danish Spiralen group, had not appeared on Cobra's international stage before.

COLLECTIVE WORKS

The essential part of Cobra's history, apart from the publications and exhibitions, lies in the contacts that were made and the meetings that took place. Despite the difficult circumstances prevailing during the years imme-

Members of Cobra at Bregneröd, 1949. From left to right: Stephen Gilbert, Simone Jaguer, Edouard Jaguer, Mrs Gilbert, Anders Österlin, Asger Jorn, Mme Dotremont, Christian Dotremont, two English architects, and (sitting) Robert Dahlman Olsen and Carl-Henning Pedersen.

diately following the war, a lot of travelling was done by members of the group. As they were all poor, and were in any case not permitted to leave their several countries with large amounts of cash, it was natural for them to stay with the artists they got to know abroad. Thus a meeting would quickly develop into a firm friendship and close collaboration.

The heart of this international meeting-ground called Cobra was what were called the *rencontres de Bregneröd* (the Bregneröd meetings). In August and September 1949 a number of Cobra members, some with their wives and children, gathered at a house in Bregneröd, just outside Copenhagen. The house had ben lent to Jorn by a group of young architects, on the condition that he would decorate the interior. They worked and lived together as one huge family, having endless discussions and painting the walls together, sometimes with the help of their children (Figs. 1 & 2). Dotremont described the whole event elaborately in the second issue of *Le Petit Cobra*. It was the realization of all those different longings and ideals which were alive in Cobra and which the members kept coming back to in their articles and manifestoes.

Influenced as they were by the theories of Marx, their hopes were centered on a new form of society in the future, where everybody would live as equals and where art would not only be for everybody but could be made by anybody. They were convinced that all people felt a need to express themselves and that this urge was suppressed and numbed by the aesthetic norms prevailing in the class structure of a capitalist society. When these aesthetic standards were eventually rejected, this "natural urge to express" would break loose and an "all-embracing people's art" would begin to blossom. Like the child and the primitive, Western man would again be able to express himself uninhibitedly. When these artists were in the process of creation, they would often let themselves be guided by the properties peculiar to, and the accidental qualities of, the materials they were using. This method of approach was for some of them consolidated by the theories of the French philosopher and psychologist Gaston Bachelard (1884-1962), who believed that matter, in the form of the four elements, was the great source of human inspiration.

In using this method of expression, the artists found that individual achievement, which had always been the centre of attention in Western culture, became devoid of all importance. The process of creation was thought to be more important than the result it produced.

Bregneröd represented the short-lived attainment of a free society in which everybody was allowed to contribute to the collective game of painting a house.

There were other occasions on which the walls of a house were painted in such a way by the members of the Cobra movement. Towards the end of 1949, Appel, Corneille and Constant left for Jutland, where they painted the interior of a house near Silkeborg which belonged to a friend of Jorn's, the trout-farmer and potter Erik Nyholm (Fig. 3). They also "improved" a geometric picture by Richard Mortensen, the result being the first of those *modifications* of which Jorn was later to create so many, using old pictures he had bought at jumble sales (Figs. 4 & 22).

This way of working together became a special characteristic of Cobra (Fig. 5). It didn't involve painters only, but more especially a combination of poets and painters through which word and image would, on impulse, be set down on a single canvas or sheet of paper (Fig. 6). The letters, words and sentences did not only add a lively pictorial element to these *peintures-mots* (word-paintings), but also communicated some poetical message. Christian Dotremont did a lot of these word-paintings, in collaboration with several of his painter friends of the movement (Figs. 7-11).

The huge web of contacts that had been established through travel, long sojourns abroad and an extensive correspondence all centred on Brussels and on Dotremont as general secretary. The *Ateliers du Marais*, in the old centre of Brussels, became the focal point of all of Cobra's activities from 1949 onwards. The building, situated in the rue du Marais, had been rented by Alechinsky and a number of his friends after they had completed their course at the *La Chambre* academy, and was promptly dubbed *The Cobra House* by Dotremont. Members from abroad would stay and work there for short periods, and all kinds of experiments were carried out, either individually or jointly. The attic housed a lithographic press on which, among other things, the lithographs for the Belgian issues of *Cobra* were printed. It was also at this house that Cobra members met other Belgian artists, whose work was sometimes to be found in Cobra exhibitions.

Les ateliers du Marais, in the rue du Marais, Brussels, 1950. Some of the inhabitants are looking out, among them (at the second-floor window in the middle) Alechinsky and his wife, Micky.

Alechinsky and his wife, Micky, working at the lithographic press in the attic of *Les ateliers du Marais*, Brussels, 1950.

THE LANGUAGE OF COBRA

Although Cobra was involved in many activities and attracted many artists, its most important contribution to modern art was the fact that it was the starting-point for the development and increasing international recognition of a number of great artists. Some, though by no means all, had for one historic moment cherished the romantic ideal of annonymous, collective labour and had, once or twice, actually been able to put it into practice. The essence of their message was that every human being had a need to express him- or herself creatively and that no rules or limitations should be imposed upon that need. Nevertheless, the artists were nothing if not pure individualists themselves. Their working methods and their uninhibited attitude did, however, bring about a change in a lot of people. The truly liberating effect of Cobra was, I think, produced by the artists' works rather than the words of its theorists and organizers.

Even though it was by no means their intention to create a new style in painting (a type of *formalism*, as they saw it), there can be no doubt that from the moment Appel, Constant and Corneille were confronted by the work of the Danish painters Carl-Henning Pedersen, Egill Jacobsen and Asger Jorn, a common style arose through mutual influences. It is not that their works are so close in style that they could be interchanged, for each clearly has his own individual style.

Their common characteristic is a direct, spontaneous way of working, using bright, unmixed colours. In the years just after the war (although the Danes were already using this method before that), the colour was applied in small patches, which were then connected by either a few clear lines or, alternatively, a confused network of many such lines. Joan Miró, the playful Surrealist, had a lot of influence on this way of composing. Within the structure of coloured specks and lines, imaginary creatures appear which look like hybrids of man, animal and plant. One should see these creatures as symbols of the desires that were alive within the movement, such as the wish to see man return to where his origins lay, with the animals and plants in nature.

There is an essential difference between the work of the Danish and the Dutch painters. That of the Danes is, in my opinion, expressive of a typically Norse attitude to nature. It does not make nature appear at all lovely or jolly, but rather as a gloomy world of strange forces in the midst of which is man. The painter's imagination conjures up creatures, gods, trolls, dwarfs and strange animals which exist beyond the limits of his ability to comprehend and around which he has spun fairy tales and myths. The work of these mythologizing artists, as featured in *Helhesten*, demands comparison with that of the Expressionists Munch and Nolde. Beyond this one feels the presence of discoveries from their own prehistory and from Scandinavian folklore, which is still very much alive. Their work can often be distinguished by an "all-over" pattern, in which no part of the canvas is left uncovered.

The Dutch felt no relation to their own prehistory, nor could they draw on a living folklore. The same desire to return to the original source of creativity led them to resort far more to children's drawings, while also turning to the work of a number of great painters of earlier generations whose influence was discernible throughout the Cobra movement. Apart from Miró, these were Picasso, Kandinsky and Klee. The work of the Dutch artists, therefore, and especially that of Constant and Appel, from the very beginning had a far more exuberant and aggressive air about it than that of the Danes, with rough, heavy lines and larger surfaces of colour, with which fantastic creatures were placed against an often empty background.

A number of the Danish members of Cobra, such as Ejler Bille and Erik Ortvad, had opted for a largely abstract style, as had the Dutch painters Theo Wolvecamp and Eugène Brands. The nucleus of the group, the ones who had conjured up a world of primeval creatures and archetypes in paint, were to develop this common language even after 1951. The childishness of the motifs and the awkwardness in design were soon to disappear. Specially in the work of Asger Jorn, who had been working in this direction since 1948 (Fig. 16), and that of Karel Appel, line and colour merge to create one wild, vehement mass of paint. From Belgium the painter Pierre Alechinsky made an important contribution to the later development of Cobra's language. Strongly influenced by Jorn as well as by Eastern calligraphy, Alechinsky developed a unique style from 1958 onwards, with which he received a place next to Appel and Jorn in international recognition (Figs. 21, 78 & 124).

In this later phase of the Cobra language, the friendly trolls and fairy-tale beings have ceased to people the canvases, their place being taken by primeval forces that have broken loose. Demonic creatures have appeared in the turbulent paint and the troubled handwriting. Something was being done about which Jorn had written to Constant in 1950: "We have to describe ourselves as animals (*bêtes humaines*)." Not until now did they abandon themselves to matter in the way they had talked about during the existence of Cobra. As far as the stylistic development of the artists is concerned, Cobra did not end in 1951.

But Cobra had been much more than just a "language" to be read in the works of a number of its members. One of the most notable characteristics of the movement was its many-sidedness, which did not only show itself in an interest in all possible disciplines in art, but also expressed itself in the activities of its members: within Cobra, poets painted and painters wrote poetry. The painters made sculptures and, when the opportunity arose, they made ceramics. So-called *objets* were put together from discarded things by painters, writers and sculptors alike. A lot of photographs were taken in which the movement is uniquely documented. Those who took them, who later became well known as photographers in their own right, such as HENNY RIEMENS (Corneille's wife) and the Belgian SERGE VANDERCAM (who later started painting in an abstract expressionist style), should also be counted among the members of Cobra.

Apart from the friction among some of the members, it was in the first place the common ideals, the close collaboration, and the expense incurred with the organization of the exhibitions and the publications, that could no longer be borne in 1951. In Belgium too many artists had become involved, so that the reasons for coming together in the same movement had become unclear. Nevertheless, it was not just the later developments in their style of painting that caused the movement to have such an important sequel; for their way of thinking, albeit sometimes in an altered form, also found a large following in movements bearing different names.

Cobra's significance for the work of its members

DENMARK

The predominantly Danish origins of Cobra can be sensed throughout the movement. Denmark also provided the most complete sequel to the movement, in the form of the activities of its great pioneer, Asger Jorn.

The work of Jorn's Danish colleagues underwent few spectacular new developments during the fifties and later. Carl-Henning Pedersen continued to extend his world of dream-birds and friendly gods and goddesses, making watercolours and oil paintings in ever larger formats, in which the stipples with which he had formerly built up his compositions became larger surfaces. He preferred to work with one dominant colour, such as white, yellow, blue or red, and sometimes a mossy brownish green (Figs. 36 & 37).

To house his work, together with that of his wife, Else Alfelt, who in her later development retained her poetical image of landscape, for which she used ever brighter colour combinations, a special museum was built in Jutland in 1975.

The paintings and sculptures of Henry Heerup, with their strong symbolic content, continued to express his extraordinary originality, his warm concern for his fellow man and his sense of humour. It is difficult, however, to distinguish particular periods or to point out specific developments in his work. Egill Jacobsen went on painting in the same style as he had started with in 1939, but his masks and plant-like beings remained fresh and direct. Ejler Bille continued to work in a poetical abstract style which he had started to develop around 1945, and which sometimes became a little ornamental. The sculptors Erik Thommesen and Sonja Ferlov both remained faithful to the direction they had set themselves in earlier years. The later works of the Icelander Svavar Gudnason show that he had exchanged his highly emotional style for a much cooler geometric abstraction.

The rather younger ERIK ORTVAD and the artist MOGENS BALLE (b. 1921), who had not joined Cobra until 1949, both, though each in his own way, developed a warm abstract style in later years, during which, especially in the case of Balle, imaginary creatures can be vaguely seen to appear (Fig. 65).

There can be no doubt that the evolution of modern Danish art during the war became known elsewhere in Europe through the initiative of the dynamic ASGER JORN. It was the first time that Danish art, which had until then been of little more than provincial importance, ventured beyond its borders, playing a pioneering role and wielding influence.

While the most important developments in the work of the majority of the Danish experimentalists took place during the years in and around the war, it was not until the fifties, after Cobra had finished, that Jorn, following his first attempts between 1945 and 1947, finally developed the dramatic and majestic style with which he attained international fame. In those years the paint was applied to the canvas with ever increasing vehemence, allowing the primordial forces of nature to burst forth in unrestrained rage. Mysterious, demonic creatures shelter among the motley shapes, while the splatters and blotches occasion-ally take on the humorous form of a somewhat confused ghost (Figs. 17-23 & 27).

Jorn experimented with all sorts of techniques. From 1953 onwards he was intensely involved with ceramics, for which he was given ample opportunity from 1954 on, at the Italian ceramic factory belonging to Tullio Mazzotti in Albisola, where he settled that year (Figs. 24-26). During that time this town became a meeting-place for a number of artists, including the old Cobra members Appel and Corneille, who began experimenting with ceramics together.

For Jorn the Cobra movement had in fact been little more than just another stage in his development as an artist, thinker and stimulating organizer. His first initiative in the last-named capacity had been the founding of *Helhesten* in 1941. In the meantime he was jotting down his thoughts on paper, publishing a series of articles and eventually even some books; and after Cobra he began to set up yet another movement in 1953. The basis for this was his loathing for functionalism in architecture, which had originated during the twenties at the Bauhaus in Germany and had subsequently dominated the postwar years. He called his new organization *Le Mouvement International pour un Bauhaus Imaginiste* (The International Movement for an Imagist Bauhaus), M.I.B.I. He was strongly supported in this by the Italian painter Enrico Baj and the young Milanese group called *The Nuclearists*, to which Baj belonged. Baj had become much impressed with the Cobra movement in 1953. Albisola and a little town slightly north of it called Alba became the centres of the new movement. Here, just as had been the case with Cobra, artists of many nationalities gathered to carry out experiments together and discuss playful living conditions in the cities of the future. In 1957 this movement, after merging with one called *Lettriste International* (represented almost exclusively by the French writer Guy Debord), was rechristened *Situationist International*. It was a widely branching movement with, among others, centres in Sweden, Belgium and Germany (*Die Gruppe Spür*). Between 1958 and 1969 it even published its own

Asger Jorn among his ceramic pieces, Albisola, 1954.

review. Jorn and Constant, who at first played leading roles in this "International," eventually distanced themselves from it in 1960, when, under the leadership of the fanatical Debord, it became more and more politically polarized, ending up as one of the major forces behind the celebrated student uprisings of 1968 in Paris.

Jorn had envisaged a rather more playful approach, and in 1962 he founded the *Scandinavian Institute for Comparative Vandalism*. It existed only on paper and its main task was to point out through publications that some cultures which were supposed to be barbaric, vandalistic or underdeveloped were by no means inferior to the so-called highly developed civilizations, of which the West was one.

In his many writings, which he worked on until just before his death in 1973, Jorn, like some twentieth-century Jean-Jacques Rousseau, pleaded continually for an environment in which Western man could have control over his own natural creativity, as was supposed to have been the case in the primeval stages of man's evolution. In the meantime he collected everything that interested him in art, especially the work of a few of his predecessors and of those contemporaries with whom he felt some affinity. This he continued to donate to the museum of Silkeborg, the town of his youth. It thus became an important centre, not only for the art of Cobra but for the whole wave of primitive expressionism which had invaded the Western world in the nineteen-fifties.

THE NETHERLANDS

Of all the countries involved, Holland was perhaps the one most drastically affected by the Cobra movement. The whole of this experimental movement, of painters as well as of poets, caused a revolution in the visual arts and the literature of the country which started with the historic years of Cobra. It was undoubtedly the inspiring force of the movement, as well as the international contacts it brought with it, that made these Dutch artists choose their own direction with such conviction in 1948. As was the case with the Danish group, the Cobra movement in Holland counted among its members a number of especially talented artists who were to win international fame.

The most conspicuous member of Cobra in Holland, with his spectacular appearances, has always been KAREL APPEL. His name was at one time even synonymous with Cobra in the Netherlands. But it was not until the mid-fifties that his fame, and with it that of Corneille, became really consolidated in Holland, thanks to the international success they were both enjoying. Appel then became so popular in his own country that he even had an impact on everyday life in the form of Appel dresses and Appel curtains.

From the beginning Appel's work had been full of vitality. He and his fellow artists had discovered their own impulsive style during the Cobra years, while living in great poverty and using cheap materials. With bright, unmixed colours he created his friendly, innocent, childlike beings and his imaginary animals (Figs. 68-71). It is noticeable, however, that particularly in that period his compositions were extremely well thought out (Figs. 72-74). In retrospect its is surprising how much hostility his work aroused in

Holland. Even a mural he had been commissioned to do in the canteen of Amsterdam's Town Hall, with the title *Questioning Children* (Fig. 72), had to be covered up with wallpaper (in which state it remained for ten years!), because the staff of the Town Hall complained that in the presence of those "questioning children" they lost their appetite completely. Appel's friend, the architect Aldo van Eyck, protested vehemently against this action with the manifesto *Een appel aan de verbeelding* (An appeal to — or an apple for — the imagination, since the Dutch word "appel" means both "apple" and "appeal"), which was stuck up on walls all over Amsterdam in 1950.

In 1950 a number of Dutch experimentalists moved out of their country, where they were not appreciated, and looked for accommodation in Paris. Appel and Corneille set up their studios in a smelly old warehouse for hides in the rue Santeuil which was ripe for demolition. They were soon joined by other artists. Appel's star began to rise in 1953, when the Parisian art promoter Michel Tapié became interested in what he was doing. From that period his work became more emotional. He could now afford better materials and larger canvases. His world of childlike creatures was devoured by the paint, which started to move around the canvas with ever increasing force. Creatures could still be discerned, making their presence felt through the vague traces of eyes and mouths, though now possessing a more demonic nature (Figs. 75-79). "I paint like a barbarian in barbaric times," he said in a film made about him in 1961 by the journalist Jan Vrijman. In this wild, violent style he painted a series of nudes and some huge portraits of several jazz musicians, as well as one of Sandberg (Figs. 76 & 77). Jazz was the music he and his friends felt closest to. Appel was an all-rounder, engaging in all possible forms of art besides painting. He made collages, sculptures in wood and later in aluminium, which he used to paint in bright colours. He received countless commissions for large-scale works in all kinds of techniques, and he even ventured into writing

DE TWIST-APPEL

Lunch op het Amsterdamse Stadhuis

Cartoon entitled *The Apple of Discord - Lunch in the Town Hall of Amsterdam*, published when the mural done by Appel in the canteen of Amsterdam's Town Hall had to be covered up because of protests from civil servants and remained hidden from view for ten years!

poetry. The extent to which this artist had upset Dutch society was put into words by Sandberg: "1949...: The name of Karel Appel — in the eyes of the good citizen — has become the symbol of rebellion."

After the exuberant start he made in 1948, CORNEILLE, when compared with the fierce, powerful Appel, seems a much quieter and more poetical character in his work. In Denmark he was much impressed by the work of Carl-Henning Pedersen, who, like Corneille, sometimes wrote poetry. Corneille spent the whole summer of 1951 with Pedersen, and in the characteristic style he began to develop at that time we find a personal version of Pedersen's large-headed creatures. These were absorbed into the sensitive play of colour and line so characteristic of his work. Paul Klee was at that time a very important influence on him (Figs. 92-96). Corneille's work often seems to be a poetically graphic account of his many wanderings. Apart from his journeys through Europe, he frequently travelled in Africa, to which he was irresistibly drawn. At first we find continual allusions to water, ships and sailing. Then, from 1950 onwards, there are compositions of labyrinthine city constructions, with a tendency to the abstract. Later still the earth's crust, increasingly emphasized, is seen in a sort of bird's-eye view.

In these compositions he repeatedly uses a round motif, in the form of a sun or a moon, or a quiet square, as a place of rest. Owing to his thoughtful way of working and his aesthetic combinations of colour, for a long time he was not seen as a Northern expressionist but was more or less assigned to the École de Paris (Figs. 97-99). At the close of the sixties his use of shape and colour became more powerful and he showed himself to be clearly inspired by the primitive art of Africa and, for example, Mexican folk art; it was then that Corneille started speaking "Cobra language" more clearly than ever before. His work in the following years was full of festively decorated birds, suns, snakes and voluptuous women in the role of mother earth, waiting and longing: the story of the constantly recurring fertility rite (Figs. 100 & 101).

CONSTANT, the committed theorist of the Dutch experimentalists and the driving force behind the group, underwent a development in his work which not only diverged from the others completely but is, even when seen alone, truly exceptional. The works of this many-sided artist are so diverse that within them one is confronted with extreme contradictions. He himself, as a convinced Marxist, explains these contradictions as stemming naturally from a dialectical alternation which, according to him, characterizes the whole of life in all its subtleties.

During the Cobra period we find the same figures borrowed from children's drawings in Constant's work as we do in that of Appel. But while in Appel's paintings they radiate uncomplicated happiness and satisfaction, in those of Constant they become frightened and aggressive beings. With his crude shapes and consciously clumsy lines, he appears to try harder than the others of the group to put into practice the anti-aestheticism propounded by Cobra (Figs. 81-83). The vehemently expressive quality he achieved was used to full advantage when, in 1950, he abandoned the fairy-tale world of Cobra and produced a series of paintings on the theme of war. Besides the mutilated bodies and the arms gesticulating desperately for help, we again find the wheels and ladders used in his fable world, but now they have been given distorted shapes (Figs. 84 & 85). For a moment the background, always present in Cobra, seems to have come to the fore, demolishing the world of fantasy in which the Cobra artists hid.

Continually preoccupied with his ideas concerning art and society, he began to concede less importance to his painting after 1952. During this period he experimented with compositions built up of large areas of colour, which he soon started to arrange in pure geometric patterns, borrowing ideas from *De Stijl*, a movement he had forcibly condemned not long before. While roaming through the great cities of London and Paris, he began to develop ideas about a playful environment for the future. He joined the *Mouvement International pour un Bauhaus Imaginiste* founded by Jorn in 1953, which he found was sympathetic to his ideas. He became an active member once more when this movement was merged in 1957 with the *Situationist International*, which had been founded that year under the leadership of the French poet Guy Debord. Together they formulated the Situationist ideal for the future which they called *Urbanisme Unitaire* (an environment in which a certain way of life and its surroundings are completely attuned to each other). Constant worked out this idea between 1956 and 1969, and the result was a series of models for a city of the future to be called *New Babylon* (Fig. 87). This "Utopia," which he regarded as a serious proposition, would materialize when technology had taken over many of man's functions, thus practically freeing him from all labour. In these new circumstances a new sort of human being would evolve, with a new sense of consciousness, freeing the suppressed creativity within him in order to become a true *homo ludens* (playing man). The way in which art functions within the traditions of Western culture in our time would then become obsolete and disappear completely.

The romantic ideal of a future in which man would "again" be free, himself, allowed to be creative, was one that was generally held among movements like Cobra. Considering all the talk of a vague past and primitive circumstances, it is remarkable that here the future was being coupled through analogy with Mondrian, for instance, or the Futurists' vision, with the advances of technology. Constant's ideas found a response in 1965 with the Provo movement in Amsterdam.

While continuing to defend his vision of the future after he had completed the *New Babylon* project, he again began to devote himself entirely to painting (Fig. 86). For a long time his subject matter remained confined to the future he had envisioned. Working in a marked expressionist style, his visions hardly convey any sense of being freed. The deserted planes containing a stilt-mounted architecture or the labyrinthine interiors divided by large partitions, in which a few figures move about, all have something of a nightmarish atmosphere about them (Fig. 88).

During the Cobra years, and while he was engaged in his *New Babylon* project, he had with great ferocity declared European culture to be finished. In the seventies, however, he consciously started to model his work on that of a number of artists from that very same European tradition (Figs. 89 & 90). To my mind this carefully executed work is reminiscent of the painters of the French and Venetian eighteenth century, with their pastel colours and decadent subject matter. Constant himself names Titian, Rubens, Delacroix and Cézanne as his great examples!

Because of their activities abroad, Appel, Constant and Corneille were called the *head* of Cobra in Holland, though other artists who had been involved with the movement argued that they were just a part of the *tail*. Nevertheless, Cobra was of fundamental importance for all of them. In the second half of the fifties, THEO WOLVECAMP started covering his canvases with heavy masses of paint in which creatures also began to make their appearance. Under the influence of the new developments initiated by Jorn and Appel, Wolvecamp began to contribute in his own way to the later phase of the "language of Cobra" (Fig. 109). Much the same may be said of ANTON ROOSKENS. During the Cobra years he had developed his own version of the language by concentrating on forms of African art and the art of the American Indians. In this version one does find some imaginary creatures, even if one's predominant feeling is of being confronted by magical signs (Figs. 102-104). From 1957 onwards, his work acquired a sombre air, with the paint spread over the canvas in large, impassioned strokes. The mythical element, which had been so important at the beginning of Cobra, suddenly reappeared in a clear and powerful figurative style in the late sixties, as had been the case with Appel and Corneille. As with them, too, the bright and cheerful colours from the Cobra period again started to gain the upper hand in Rooskens' work (Fig. 105).

The work of JAN NIEUWENHUYS was dominated in the Cobra period by a figurative style partly based on children's drawings which, rather than consciously naive or childish, has something of alienation about it, rather like what we find in the work of the Surrealist Victor Brauner (Fig. 107). The same feeling prevails in Nieuwenhuys' later, largely abstract work, with its harsh colours and the thread-like shapes moving the paint around the canvas.

During his short-lived participation in Cobra, EUGÈNE BRANDS worked in a lyrical abstract way (Fig. 110). When, in 1950, he seemed taken with the figuration of Cobra, having discovered children's drawings as a source of inspiration, he singled out its magical element and brought it to the foreground. Up to 1960 he produced a large series of paintings in oil on paper or canvas in which he created a mysterious world of signs: a lock and key,

arrows, unattached legs wandering into the composition from above, hands, floating ships, etc. (Figs. 111 & 112). He continued with this secretive world of signs in his more abstract, though sometimes surreal, reliefs (Fig. 113).

Everything in his work is characterized by his personal "woolly" or "smudgy" application of paint. It was after 1960 that he began to develop this technique, using increasingly large canvases and creating a lyrical spatial language in which his particular use of such colours as orange, white, yellow, clear green and light blue is rather conspicuous. In this later work Brands also wanted to express the magical forces which connect everything with everything else throughout the cosmos (Fig. 114).

The Cobra movement was of tremendous importance for the poet and painter LUCEBERT, even though he was only indirectly involved with it and for but a short time. On the one hand, Cobra stimulated him and his fellow experimental poets, Gerrit Kouwenaar and Jan Elburg, to find the freedom in language they had been searching for and to use that freedom with conviction; on the other, the movement made a deep impression on him as a painter.

The experimental poets in the Netherlands formed a parallel movement to Cobra, calling themselves the "Vijftigers" ("Fifty-ers"). Like the painters, they may be said to have used the irrational world of Surrealism in an expressionist way. These poets, among whom there where some who had not been involved with Cobra at all, used the same spontaneous, improvising approach to their material. They often let themselves be guided by associations, unusual meanings or coincidental combinations of, for example, sounds which the language itself provided.

From an early age the "Emperor of the Fifty-ers," as a critic called LUCEBERT in 1953, had occupied himself with both painting and drawing besides his poetry. He managed to raise a lot of dust with his performances and his poetry, and subsequently he received a good deal of recognition in his own country as well as from abroad. Like so many of the Cobra painters, he is a "mythomaniac." The mythology he creates, both in painting and in poetry, is more directly concerned with the world of people than that of the others, and it is full of literary allusions. In 1948 he became fascinated by the work of Picasso and Miró. But not until 1952 do we find in his drawings and gouaches those mythical creatures so clearly related

(a) Shinkichi Tajiri's studio in Paris, around 1952.

(b) Lotti van der Gaag with one of her sculptures (later destroyed) in the rue Santeuil, Paris, 1951.

to the ones that peopled the works done in that period by some of his Cobra friends. To these works he gave names like *Daedalus* or *Orpheus and the Animals*, which was something those friends would never have dreamt of doing (Figs. 115 & 116). Lucebert underwent a lot of different influences during the fifties. A constant characteristic of his work is the poetical play of line and colour, in which he lets himself be guided by coincidence. Around 1960, the "old mythologizing language" of Cobra started to dominate his work (Figs. 117 & 118). He became fascinated by the figurative quality of Cobra, reminiscent of children's drawings. Soon the childlike and the good-natured disappeared, making way for a caricatural, demonic vision of the world of people. During the sixties his style became increasingly harsh and aggressive. With unsparing ferocity he depicted man possessed by his own passions (Fig. 119).

The American sculptor SHINKICHI TAJIRI (*b.* 1923), who was born of Japanese parents, had come into contact with the Cobra group in Paris in 1949, and more particularly with its Dutch members, which eventually led him to settle in Holland permanently in 1956.

A link can be discerned between the work of Tajiri's Cobra friends and his own spatial experiments with organic forms and refuse at that time (Fig. 121). The work of Calder must have been of some importance to him in this. The basic form characteristic of many of his sculptures is a fantastic structure on high, slender supports, which in the fifties represented the aggressive figure of a warrior. Later on, during the sixties, he stopped using the rough, spiny finish that belonged to that period. From then on he gave preference to perfection in shape and smoothly polished surfaces.

In the winter of 1950-51 the sculptress LOTTI VAN DER GAAG (*b.* 1923) joined the circle of Dutch Cobra members who had moved to Paris. On arriving from The Hague she moved into the hide warehouse in the rue Santeuil. Her frightening half-animal half-human creatures, which she had been producing in clay and plaster since 1948-49, fitted in with Cobra's language very well. Within the open shapes which became characteristic of her work after she had been taking lessons from Zadkine in Paris for a short time, vegetable growths can be discerned after 1951 which gradually take over from the imaginary beings (Fig. 120). It can be clearly seen that she also felt closely related to Cobra when she started painting in the mid-sixties.

BELGIUM

In Belgium, which was the organizational centre of Cobra, the significance of the movement was different from what it had been for Denmark and the Netherlands. Dotremont, who as general secretary probably felt that he bore the ultimate responsibility for the review, must for a long time have thought of Cobra as being primarily a militant red *International* of artists. He put everything he had into its organization. Years later he wrote about the effort it had cost him: "....The poverty, then the illness! Think of it, Cobra published a score of reviews and the *Bibliothèque de Cobra* in three years!....Without any money!....The vitality, the daring, the stubbornness, the hunger that as it were created Cobra: that is important!"

Cobra's ideal of allowing everyone's creativity free rein found the greatest response in Belgium. The building in the rue du Marais became a hive of activity; painters, sculptors, writers, poets, film-makers, photographers all indulged their creativity, neither keeping to their own speciality nor obeying any rules whatsoever.

The fact that this complete freedom had nothing to do with the attitude of the Communist Party in Russia to the arts was not actually discovered by Dotremont until the autumn of 1949. It was then that a lot of people in the West, who had felt themselves to be closely associated with the Communist world, were suddenly confronted with the strangling demands of Socialist Realism, which the Soviet Union had imposed on the artist since 1934 as the only direction open to him. The enraged Dotremont, followed almost at once by Alechinsky, left the Communist Party in October 1949. He then aired his indignation in a pamphlet entitled *Le réalisme socialiste contre la révolution* (Socialist Realism against the Revolution). It appeared as a Cobra publication in Brussels in 1950.

The openness to all sides, which led many artists, albeit often for only a short time, to join the Belgian branch of Cobra without being really aware of its international character, made *Cobra-Belgium* a rather heterogeneous movement.

It comes as no surprise that during that time Belgium contributed little to the characteristic expressions of Cobra. Artistic production in Belgium was dominated on the one hand by the Surrealists, including older writers like Marcel Havrenne and the younger Dotremont and Joseph Noiret, the film-makers Jean Raine and Luc Zangrie (Luc de Heusch), the painter-sculptor Pol Bury, and the architect-draughtsman Paul Bourgoignie. On the other hand it was led by the Jeune Peinture Belge group, which included most of the artists who had had some involvement with Cobra in those years. Among these were the painters Raoul Ubac, Louis van Lint, Georges Collignon, Jan Cox (Fig. 134) and, lastly, Pierre Alechinsky. A number of these artists were much influenced by the lyrical abstract work of the French painter Jean Bazaine, a prominent member of the École de Paris; Alechinsky, in fact, gave Bazaine a place of honour in the last Cobra exhibition, held in Liège in October and November 1951. The work of most of these Belgian artists followed trends in art which already existed in Belgium, trends from which the Danes and the Dutch were in fact trying to dissociate themselves! Although Dotremont and Alechinsky, like the Dutch, were strongly attracted to Denmark, it was not until 1960 that the Belgians found their own version of the visual language in which the Danes and the Dutch had found each other long before. It was especially in the work of Pierre Alechinsky that they did so.

Where Belgium did make an important contribution to the visual expression of Cobra was in the collaboration of poets and painters, in which handwriting was used as a pictorial element in the composition. This form of collaboration had been strongly stimulated by Dotremont. He himself produced a large series of these *peintures-mots* with Asger Jorn between 1947 and 1953 (Figs. 7 & 8). He also worked with, among others, Atlan, Corneille, Alechinsky and the Flemish writer-painter HUGO CLAUS (*b.* 1929), who had had some contacts with Cobra (Figs. 9-11 & 135). After 1951 he continued this activity with many of his old Cobra friends (Figs. 133 & 136). At first the texts used by Dotremont expressed a clear poetical message, using a characteristic play on words which he also exploited in his prose texts, whether in the form of manifestoes, commentaries or descriptions of the art of his colleagues. At length his interest in the calligraphic element became predominant, much of his work being influenced by Eastern calligraphy. In 1962, Dotremont abandoned poetry for painting. The calligraphy he produced from then on started out from an existing word or text, which was, however, illegible. These works he called *Logogrammes* (Figs. 131 & 132).

ALECHINSKY had also at an early stage become fascinated by personal handwriting as well as Eastern calligraphy. During the Cobra years, such diverse interests as medieval woodcuts, the work of the Belgian painter Edgar Tijtgat and that of Bazaine had all been sources of inspiration to him (Figs. 122 & 123). After his introduction to Cobra he threw himself with such enthusiasm into the organization of the movement — in the course of which the review and the rebuilding of the studios in the rue du Marais demanded most of his attention — that he had little time to devote to his own work. This did not really take off until after Cobra had ended. In 1955 he made a journey to Japan, where he studied calligraphy and even made a film about it.

Alechinsky's largely abstract style gradually became wilder and more thickly impastoed during the second half of the fifties. He covered his canvases with what looked like a teeming mass of maggots in predominantly white, grey, green and blue tones (Fig. 124). Around 1958, imaginary creatures began to make their appearance. Daring to use even greater freedom in colour and form, he made a very specific contribution to the "mythologizing language" of Cobra (Figs. 125-127). In this work he was chiefly inspired by Asger Jorn and Eastern calligraphy.

As from the mid-sixties, he expressed himself almost exclusively on paper, which he then stuck on to a canvas. He worked like an Eastern calligrapher, bent over the paper lying on the floor. Using ink and — from 1965 onwards — acrylic paint, with quick movements of the brush he created monstrous creatures which sometimes addressed each other, as in a strip cartoon. On the one hand his work is characterized by the (calligraphic) speed at which he worked and the transparent clarity of the colours he used; on the other, in conjuring up these figures

Alechinsky appears to be holding up a distorting mirror to the viewer, reminding one of his great Flemish predecessors, James Ensor, Hieronymus Bosch and Pieter Brueghel, to all of whom he renders homage in the titles of his works (Figs. 128-130).

After 1960, Alechinsky became increasingly interested in collaborating with other artists. From then on publications appeared almost every year with poetical texts by various authors, such as Dotremont, but also by Alechinsky himself, which he illustrated with his humorous fairy-tale creatures.

Very few of the artists concerned with Cobra in Belgium were later to contribute to what is here called Cobra's "language". Among those who did were JEAN RAINE (*b.* 1927) and REINHOUD D'HAESE (*b.* 1928), both of them good friends of Alechinsky. Raine was at first especially interested in cinema, but in 1962 he started painting in a style reminiscent of Alechinsky's. The sculptor Reinhoud, who had helped in the work of converting the studios in the rue du Marais in 1949, did not really take off in his work until 1958. From then on, using different sorts of metal or, on a smaller scale, bread, he produced a whole population of mysterious and humorous imaginary creatures which fitted in completely with the Cobra family (Figs. 137 & 138).

OTHER COUNTRIES

Of the other countries taking part in Cobra, albeit with few artists, France played the most important role. The painters Atlan and Doucet both contributed actively to the movement, each in his own way, while their work also fitted in well. The support of the writers and critics Jaguer and Ragon was of great importance to the group. Even after 1951 they continued to show their interest in the movement in their published work. In his violent expressionist style, JEAN-MICHEL ATLAN (1913-1960) started in 1947-48 to conjure up a swampy, vegetative world of creatures partaking equally of the characteristics of plants, animals and humans. Looking at this work, one is reminded of dancing warriors and magical signs. In his

Ma raison n'est pas ma maison (My Reason is not My Home) (Text by Christian Dotremont, drawing by Pierre Alechinsky), 1950, gouache and ink on paper, 34.5×50 cm, unsigned. Collection Alechinsky.

REINHOUD: *Mies de pain (foule)*. Bread crumbs (crowd). 1962. Some that survived are cast in silver or bronze. Collection of the artist.

later development, these signs assumed vigorous ornamental forms (Figs. 11, 139 & 140). JACQUES DOUCET (*b*. 1924) had tried to find his own style, in which he took Paul Klee and Miró as his examples (Fig. 141). He formed a special relationship with the Dutch members of the group. During the fifties he developed a warm abstract style in his collages and paintings. In the latter the paint is elaborately interwoven, spreading over the surface of the canvas like a large, sluggish, organic mass (Fig. 142).

Edouard Jaguer wrote several articles about members of the movement for publications like the *Bibliothèque de Cobra*. He also contributed poems to the review *Cobra* and, through his extensive contacts in the international art world, was able to provide *Le Petit Cobra* with a lot of interesting information. In 1954 he started the publication of a review called *Phases*, in which he presented various artists he had met through Cobra and at the same time kept in touch with Jorn's new *International Movement for an Imagist Bauhaus*. Michel Ragon, a friend and great admirer of Atlan, was one of the first of the few critics to take an early interest in Cobra. In 1969 he published his memoirs of the years spent with Cobra in a book entitled *Vingt-cinq ans d'art vivant*.

Something remained in Cobra from the contacts that the Franco-Belgian Revolutionary Surrealist Movement had made with a group in Czechoslovakia called *Ra*, though the only member of that group to take part in any of Cobra's activities was the painter JOSEPH ISTLER. With a Czechoslovakian Surrealist movement as background, Istler is said to have developed a style in those years which, as far as can be deduced from an article on those Czech artists written by Edouard Jaguer in 1965 for his review *Phases*, was half-way between lyrical abstraction and the fantastic.

For the German painter KARL OTTO GÖTZ (*b*. 1914), his first contact with Cobra, in 1949, was of lasting significance. In his completely battered country, where modern art had been obliterated by the Nazi régime, Götz had been busy trying to acquire information about the latest developments, in poetry as well as the visual arts, in Germany and elsewhere. Everything he found was printed in a tiny review called *META* which he published from 1948 to 1953 under the pseudonym André Tamm. He accepted with great enthusiasm the invitation to participate in the 1949 Cobra exhibition in Amsterdam. But there is little relation between Götz's work and the uninhibited expressionism of so many Cobra artists. On the one hand he made Surrealist-inspired experiments in monoprinting (Fig. 145); on the other, he made series of compositions using paint or woodcut, with smooth abstract shapes reminiscent of the work of Hans Arp. In the fifties he developed a style which the wild brushwork almost justifies us in describing as abstract expressionist, but which, thanks to his method of working at great speed with huge brushes, comes over as cold and mechanical.

The Englishman STEPHEN GILBERT (*b*. 1910), whose work had been discovered by Jorn at the Salon des Surindépendants in Paris, had produced, while on a visit to Ireland during the war, a series of paintings with strange winged creatures, ghostly spiders and huge dragonflies, which fitted in well with Cobra ideas (Fig. 143). Having joined the movement, he took part in a lot of its activities with great enthusiasm, becoming particularly friendly with Constant. In 1949 he started working in an abstract style and in the fifties he chose a completely different medium for expressing himself, becoming a sculptor in metal, in which he endeavoured to produce pure, harmonious forms. Gilbert's friend, the English painter WILLIAM GEAR (*b*. 1915), had met several members of Cobra in Paris and he, too, though with less conviction, took part in Cobra manifestations. The work he did at that time could be called abstract expressionist (Fig. 144). He later developed a style which was of a cooler, more rationalist character.

Soon after the war, contacts had been established between the Danish painters of the *Höst* group and a number of Swedish artists who had formed a group of a markedly Surrealist character called *Imaginisterna*. A few of these Swedes, particularly the painters ANDERS ÖSTERLIN (*b*. 1926) and CARL OTTO HULTÉN (*b*. 1916), were to devote some attention to Cobra. The enthusiasm felt for Cobra in their circle, however, was not very great. Österlin's poetical work of the years immediately after the war was inspired by Paul Klee and specific forms of folk art (Fig. 147). In his later, predominantly abstract work, he plays with interconnecting planes, giving his work something of the character of collage. Of all these Swedish artists, Hultén was perhaps the one most closely related to the Cobra painters, with the radical expressionism he developed after his Surrealist start (Fig. 146). In the years following the war, imaginary creatures began to appear in his painting, but later he chose a more abstract style. The work of MAX WALTER SVANBERG (*b*. 1912), who also belonged to the group that had maintained contacts with Cobra, has a more surreal air about it. Using a minutely detailed ornamental style, he creates fantastic dreamlike visions in which strange female figures play the leading roles and horrifying monsters appear (Fig. 148).

The Hungarian-born ZOLTAN KEMENY and his wife, MADELEINE ZEMERE KEMENY, represented Switzerland, their adopted country, at the big Cobra exhibition in Amsterdam in 1949. Their primitivist work of that period had been discovered by Corneille at a little gallery in Paris and was well attuned to the spirit of Cobra. They had, however, no real contact with the movement, nor did they seek any.

Cobra editorial meeting at Atlan's studio in Paris. From left to right: Doucet, Constant, Dotremont, Mme Atlan, Atlan, Corneille, Appel.

Conclusion

Cobra was a movement typically belonging to those few years immediately after the Second World War, when the Cold War had as yet hardly made itself felt. In its spontaneity, and with its utopian visions, Cobra visualized and voiced that moment when naive optimism could still exist, when extravagant and romantic expectations of the near future could still be indulged. When, in November 1951, Cobra came to an end with the publication of the tenth and last issue of the review, the realization of the Cold War's existence had penetrated deeply, leaving Cobra behind as no more than an island of dreams, a brief and ingenuous past. The simple mythical creatures that had been produced in that period were later to be lost in the dramatic violence of subsequent painting. On that island of dreams, which in fact lasted no longer than a year and a half (from 1948 to 1950), the occupations which the Surrealists had regarded as no more than research experiments or games were put on a truly creative level. Automatism became spontaneity; and not only that, but also the anonymous collective, that is to say the collaboration of several partners, ceased to be just an intriguing party game, like the Surrealists' *cadavre exquis*, and became instead a real creative experience.

Nevertheless, Cobra was to have a sequel in various ways. On the one hand, its ideals were perpetuated in the movements started by Jorn and in the collective happenings organized mostly by Dotremont, as well as others. On the other, interest was created in the movement through the fame attained by some of its painter members with the later development of their work. For with this subsequent evolution of their several styles these artists formed part of the wave of vehement emotion in paint that swept the fifties like an epidemic. The painters of Cobra, however, remained recognizable in the mythical figuration repeatedly breaking through in their work.

A primeval longing, of the sort that had made Jean-Jacques Rousseau exclaim "Back to nature!" in the second half of the eighteenth century, had burst out in their painting with greater vehemence than ever. Now that the Industrial Revolution had gone so far that just one push of a button could destroy the whole of nature, the call back to nature had become the desire of a worldwide movement in art. And this call was not in fact silenced, but was taken up by the provo, flower-power and hippy movements of the sixties.

Jorn wrote to Constant in 1950: "I work with the primordial cells from which life itself originated, in the days when it all began." With these words Jorn formulated all that which had obsessed this vital and dramatic postwar generation of artists.

Alechinsky and Appel working together in Alechinsky's studio in Paris (Bougival), 1976-77. Their joint work of that period was published in Paris in 1978, in a book entitled *Encre à deux pinceaux*, with poems by Hugo Claus. (Dutch edition published by Landshoff, 1978.)

MANIFESTO

The dissolution of Western Classical culture is a phenomenon that can be understood only against the background of a social evolution which can end only in the total collapse of a principle of society thousands of years old and its replacement by a system whose laws are based on the immediate demands of human vitality. The influence the ruling classes have wielded over the creative consciousness in history has reduced art to an increasingly dependent position, until finally the real psychic function of that art was attainable only for a few spirits of genius who in their frustration and after a long struggle were able to break out of the conventions of form and rediscover the basic principles of all creative activity.

Together with the class society from which it emerged, this culture of the individual is faced by destruction too, as the former's institutions, kept alive artificially, offer no further opportunities for the creative imagination and only impede the free expression of human vitality. All the isms so typical of the last fifty years of art history represent so many attempts to bring new life to this culture and to adapt its aesthetic to the barren ground of its social environment. Modern art, suffering from a permanent tendency to the constructive, an obsession with objectivity (brought on by the disease that has destroyed our speculative-idealizing culture), stands isolated and powerless in a society which seems bent on its own destruction. As the extension of a style created for a social elite, with the disappearance of that elite modern art has lost its social justification and is confronted only by the criticism formulated by a clique of connoisseurs and amateurs.

Western art, once the celebrator of emperors and popes, turned to serve the newly powerful bourgeoisie, becoming an instrument of the glorification of bourgeois ideals. Now that these ideals have become a fiction with the disappearance of their economic base, a new era is upon us, in which the whole matrix of cultural conventions loses its significance and a new freedom can be won from the most primary source of life. But, just as with a social revolution, this spiritual revolution cannot be enacted without conflict. Stubbornly the bourgeois mind clutches on to its aesthetic ideal and in a last, desperate effort employs all its wiles to convert the indifferent masses to the same belief. Taking advantage of the general lack of interest, suggestions are made of a special social need for what is referred to as "an ideal of beauty", all designed to prevent the flowering of a new, conflicting sense of beauty which emerges from the vital emotions.

As early as the end of World War I the DADA movement tried by violent means to break away from the old ideal of beauty. Although this movement concentrated increasingly on the political arena, as the artists involved perceived that their struggle for freedom brought them into conflict with the laws that formed the very foundations of society, the vital power released by this confrontation also stimulated the birth of a new artistic vision.

In 1924 the Surrealist Manifesto appeared, revealing a hitherto hidden creative impulse — it seemed that a new source of inspiration had been discovered. But BRETON's movement suffocated in its own intellectualism, without ever converting its basic principle into a tangible value. For Surrealism was an art of ideas and as such also infected by the disease of past class culture, while the movement failed to destroy the values this culture proclaimed in its own justification.

It is precisely this act of destruction that forms the key to the liberation of the human spirit from passivity. It is the basic pre-condition for the flowering of a people's art that encompasses everyone. The general social impotence, the passivity of the masses, are an indication of the brakes that cultural norms apply to the natural expression of the forces of life. For the satisfaction of this primitive need for vital expression is the driving force of life, the cure for every form of vital weakness. It transforms art into a power for spiritual health. As such it is the property of all and for this reason every limitation that reduces art to the preserve of a small group of specialists, connoisseurs and virtuosi must be removed.

But this people's art is not an art that necessarily conforms to the norms set by the people, for they expect what they were brought up with, unless they have had the opportunity to experience something different. In other words, unless the people themselves are actively involved in the making of art. A people's art is a form of expression nourished only by a natural and therefore general urge to expression. Instead of solving problems posed by some preconceived aesthetic ideal, this art recognizes only the norms of expressivity, spontaneously directed by its own intuition. The great value of a people's art is that, precisely because it is the form of expression of the untrained, the greatest possible latitude is given to the unconscious, thereby opening up ever wider perspectives for the comprehension of the secret of life. In the art of genius, too, Western Classical culture has recognized the value of the unconscious, for it was the unconscious which made possible a partial liberation from the conventions which bound art. But this could be achieved only after a long, personal process of development, and was always seen as revolutionary. The cycle of revolutionary deeds which we call the evolution of art has now entered its last phase: the loosening of stylistic conventions. Already weakened by Impressionism, laid bare by Cubism (and later by Constructivism and Neo-Plasticism), it signifies the end of art as a force of aesthetic idealism on a higher plane than life. What we call "genius" is nothing else but the power of the individual to free himself from the ruling aesthetic and place himself above it. As this aesthetic loses its stranglehold, and with the disappearance of the exceptional personal performance, "genius" will become public property and the word "art" will acquire a completely new meaning. That is not to say that the expression of all people will take on a similar, generalized value, but that everyone will be able to express himself because the genius of the people, a fountain in which everyone can bathe, replaces the individual performance.

In this period of change, the role of the creative artist can only be that of the revolutionary: it is his duty to destroy the last remnants of an empty, irksome aesthetic, arousing the creative instincts still slumbering unconscious in the human mind. The masses, brought up with aesthetic conventions imposed from without, are as yet unaware of their creative potential. This will be stimulated by an art which does not define but suggests, by the arousal of associations and the speculations which come forth from them, creating a new and fantastic way of seeing. The onlooker's creative ability (inherent to human nature) will bring this new way of seeing within everyone's reach once aesthetic conventions cease to hinder the working of the unconscious.

Hitherto condemned to a purely passive role in our culture, the onlooker will himself become involved in the creative process. The interaction between creator and observer makes art of this kind a powerful stimulator in the birth of the creativity of the people. The ever greater dissolution and ever more overt impotence of our culture makes the struggle of today's creative artists easier than that of their predecessors — time is on their side. The phenomenon of "kitsch" has spread so quickly that today it overshadows more cultivated forms of expression, or else is so intimately interwoven with them that a demarcation line is difficult to draw. Thanks to these developments, the power of the old ideals of beauty are doomed to decay and eventually disappear and a new artistic principle, now coming into being, will automatically replace them. This new principle is based on the total influence of matter on the creative spirit. This creative concept is not one of theories or forms, which could be described as solidified matter, but arises from the confrontation between the human spirit and raw materials that suggest forms and ideas.

Every definition of form restricts the material effect and with it the suggestion it projects. Suggestive art is materialistic art because only matter stimulates creative activity, while the more perfectly defined the form, the less active is the onlooker. Because we see the activation of the urge to create as art's most

important task, in the coming period we will strive for the greatest possible materialistic and therefore greatest possible suggestive effect. Viewed in this light, the creative act is more important than that which it creates, while the latter will gain in significance the more it reveals the work which brought it into being and the less it appears as a polished end-product. The illusion has been shattered that a work of art has a fixed value: its value is dependent on the creative ability of the onlooker, which in turn is stimulated by the suggestions the work of art arouses. Only living art can activate the creative spirit, and only living art is of general significance. For only living art gives expression to the emotions, yearnings, reactions and ambitions which as a result of society's shortcomings we all share.

A living art makes no distinction between beautiful and ugly because it sets no aesthetic norms. The ugly which in the art of past centuries has come to supplement the beautiful is a permanent complaint against the unnatural class society and its aesthetic of virtuosity; it is a demonstration of the retarding and limiting influence of this aesthetic on the natural urge to create. If we observe forms of expression that include every stage of human life, for example that of a child (who has yet to be socially integrated), then we no longer find this distinction. The child knows of no law other than its spontaneous sensation of life and feels no need to express anything else. The same is true of primitive cultures, which is why they are so attractive to today's human beings, forced to live in a morbid atmosphere of unreality, lies and infertility. A new freedom is coming into being which will enable human beings to express themselves in accordance with their instincts. This change will deprive the artist of his special position and meet with stubborn resistance. For, as his individually won freedom becomes the possession of all, the artist's entire individual and social status will be undermined.

Our art is the art of a revolutionary period, simultaneously the reaction of a world going under and the herald of a new era. For this reason it does not conform to the ideals of the first, while those of the second have yet to be formulated. But it is the expression of a life force that is all the stronger for being resisted, and of considerable psychological significance in the struggle to establish a new society. The spirit of the bourgeoisie still permeates all areas of life, and now and then it even pretends to bring art to the people (a special people, that is, set to its hand).

But this art is too stale to serve as a drug any longer. The chalkings on pavements and walls clearly show that human beings were born to manifest themselves; now the struggle is in full swing against the power that would force them into the straitjacket of clerk or commoner and deprive them of this first vital need. A painting is not a composition of colour and line but an animal, a night, a scream, a human being, or all of these things together. The objective, abstracting spirit of the bourgeois world has reduced the painting to the means which brought it into being; the creative imagination, however, seeks to recognize every form *and even in the sterile environment of the abstract it has created a new relationship with reality, turning on the suggestive power which every natural or artificial form possesses for the active onlooker. This suggestive power knows no limits and so one can say that after a period in which it meant NOTHING, art has now entered an era in which it means EVERYTHING.*

The cultural vacuum has never been so strong or so widespread as after the last war, when the continuity of centuries of cultural evolution was broken by a single jerk of the string. The Surrealists, who in their rejection of the cultural order threw artistic expression overboard, experienced the disillusionment and bitterness of talent become useless in a destructive campaign against art, against a society which, though they recognized its responsibility, was still strong enough to be considered as theirs. However, painters after World War II see themselves confronted by a world of stage decors and false façades in which all lines of communication have been cut and all belief has vanished. The total lack of a future as a continuation of this world makes constructive thought impossible. Their only salvation is to turn their backs on the entire culture (including modern negativism, Surrealism and Existentialism). In this process of liberation it becomes increasingly apparent that this culture, unable to make artistic expression possible, can only make it impossible. The materialism of these painters did not lead, as bourgeois idealists had warned, to a spiritual void (like their own?), nor to creative impotence. On the contrary, for the first time every faculty of the human spirit was activated in a fertile relationship with matter. At the same time a process was started in which ties and specific cultural forms which in this phase still played a role were naturally thrown off, just as they were in other areas of life.

The problematic phase in the evolution of modern art has come to an end and is being followed by an experimental period. In other words, from the experience gained in this state of unlimited freedom, the rules are being formulated which will govern the new form of creativity. Come into being more or less unawares, in line with the laws of dialectics a new consciousness will follow.

CONSTANT NIEUWENHUYS
Published in *Reflex* I, Amsterdam, September-October 1948

Translated from the Dutch by Leonard Bright

Select Bibliography

1951

RAGON, Michel: *Expression et nonfiguration*, Ed. de la Revue Neuf, Robert Delpire, Paris, 1951.

1957

PEDERSEN, Carl-Henning: *Universum Fabularum*, (En indföring i hans billedverden), with a text by C.H. Pedersen and an introduction in Danish and French by Erik Andreasen. Munksgaard, Copenhagen, 1957.

1958

ALLOWAY, Lawrence: "Cobra Notes," Background to action (a series of six articles on postwar painting), No. 5, *Art News and Review*, 4 January 1958, Vol. IX, No. 25.

1960

CATALOGUE of the exhibition "Cobra 1960," Lefèbre Gallery, New York, November/December 1960. Introduction by H.L.C. Jaffé.

1961

VAD, Poul: *Ejler Bille*, (text in Danish and English). Munksgaard, Copenhagen, 1961.

CATALOGUE of the exhibition "Cobra dix ans après," Galerie Mathias Fels, Paris, May/June 1961. Introduction by Michel Ragon.

1962

BEEREN, W.A.L.: "Het Cobra schilderij (Notities over moderne kunst III)," *Hollands Weekblad*, 3rd year, No. 138, 24 January 1962, pp 14 ff.

CLAUS, Hugo: *Karel Appel painter*, A.J.G. Strengholt, Amsterdam, 1962. (Pocket edition in Dutch, 1964).

DOTREMONT, Chr.: "Cobra," in *L'Œil*, December 1962, No. 96, pp 56 ff.

Het Museumjournaal (journaal van de Nederlandse musea voor moderne kunst), 7th series, No. 7/8, 1962 (devoted entirely to the Cobra movement, with contributions by Troels Andersen, Christian Dotremont, Gerrit Kouwenaar, J. Martinet, J. Eykelboom & Wim Beeren).

RAGON, Michel: *Atlan*, Georges Fall Éditeur, Paris, 1962.

WILMAN, Preben: *Heerup*, (text in Danish and English). Munksgaard, Copenhagen, 1962.

1963

DOTREMONT, Christian: *Egill Jacobsen*, (text in Danish and French). Munksgaard, Copenhagen, 1963.

VINKENOOG, Simon: *Karel Appel*, A.W. Bruna & Zoon, Utrecht, 1963.

CATALOGUE of the exhibition "Visione e Colore," Centro Internazionale delle Arti e del Costume, Palazzo Grassi, Venice, 6 July to 6 October 1963. Introduction by Paolo Marinotti.

1964

ATKINS, Guy and SCHMIDT, Erik: *Bibliografi over Asger Jorns Skrifter til 1963*, Privattryk, Permild & Rosengreen, Copenhagen, 1964.

ATKINS, Guy (ed.): *Asger Jorn's Aarhus Mural*, texts by Guy Atkins and Erik Nyholm. Westerham Press, Kent, England, 1964.

VAD, Poul: *Erik Thommesen*, (text in Danish and English). Munksgaard, Copenhagen, 1964.

1965

THORSEN, Jens Jorgen: *Modernisme i Dansk Kunst, specielt efter 1940*, Ed. Thanig & Appel, Copenhagen, 1965.

SCHADE, Virtus: *Asger Jorn*. Stig Vendelkaers Forlag, Copenhagen, 1965.

1966

SCHADE, Virtus: *Carl-Henning Pedersen*. Stig Vendelkaers Forlag, Copenhagen, 1966.

CATALOGUE of the exhibition "Cobra 1948-1951," Museum Boymans-van Beuningen, Rotterdam, 20 May to 17 July 1966. Catalogue and exhibition by Willemijn Stokvis (de Haas).

Louisiana Revy, 7th year, No, 1, August 1966. This issue was used as the catalogue for an exhibition of Cobra works held at the Louisiana Museum, Humlebaek, Denmark from 19 August to 20 October 1966. Apart from a few additions, the exhibition and the catalogue were exactly as in Rotterdam earlier in the same year.

1967

JESPERSEN, Gunnar: *De abstrakte (Linien, Helhesten, Höstudstillingen, Cobra)*, Berlinske Forlag, Copenhagen, 1967.

PUTMAN, Jacques: *Pierre Alechinsky*. Fratelli Fabbri, Milan. Odège, Paris, 1967.

SCHADE, Virtus: *Heerup*. Stig Vendelkaers Forlag, Copenhagen, 1967.

1968

ATKINS, Guy: *Jorn in Scandinavia, 1930-1953*, Lund Humphries, London, 1968.

1969

RAGON, Michel: *Vingt-cinq ans d'art vivant, Chronique vécue de l'art contemporain/de l'abstraction au popart*, Casterman, Tournai, Belgium, 1969.

CATALOGUE of the exhibition "Lucebert, Schilderijen, gouaches, tekeningem en grafiek," Stedelijk Museum, Amsterdam, 19 April to 1 June 1969.

1970

HEUSCH, Luc de: *Reinhoud*, Fratelli Pozzo, Turin, 1970.

1971

SCHADE, Virtus: *Cobra —fra hoved til hale*, Copenhagen, 1971. (In Dutch translation, published 1972, Ghent, Belgium).

1973

ALECHINSKY, Pierre: *Les Estampes de 1946 à 1972*, (Catalogue raisonné). Yves Rivières, Paris, 1973.

LAUDE, André: *Corneille, Le Roi-Image*. Éditions S.M.I., Paris, 1973.

1974

CATALOGUE of the exhibition "Cobra 48-51-74," in the Town Hall of Brussels, 4-28 April, 1974.

STOKVIS, Willemijn: *Cobra. Geschiedenis, voorspel en betekenis van een beweging in de kunst van na de tweede wereldoorlog* (Doctoral Thesis), De Bezige Bij, Amsterdam, 1974. 2nd edition 1980, 3rd edition 1985.

JESPERSEN, Gunnar: *Cobra*, Gyldendal, Denmark, 1974.

CONSTANT: *New Babylon*, with an introduction by J.L. Locher. Published at the occasion of an exhibition in the Municipal Museum of The Hague, Netherlands, 15 June-1 September 1974.

1975

LOREAU, Max: *Dotremont, Logogrammes*. Éditions Georges Fall, Paris, 1975.

MAURIZI, Elverio: *L'Opera grafica di Corneille, 1948-1974*. Introduction by Georges Boudaille (in Italian and French). La Nuova Foglio Editrice, 1975.

1976

WINGEN, Ed.: *Rooskens*. Van Spijk, Venlo, 1976.

1977

ATKINS, Guy: *Asger Jorn, The Crucial Years: 1954-1964*, Lund Humphries, London, 1977.

BANDINI, Mirella: *L'Estetico/Il Politico, da Cobra all'Internazionale Situazionista 1948-1957*, Officina Edizioni, Rome, 1977.

1979

CATALOGUE of the exhibition "Eugène Brands," (travelling to different cities in Holland, 1979-1981), with an introduction by Willemijn Stokvis. Edition Galerie Nouvelles Images, The Hague, Netherlands.

1980

ATKINS, Guy: *Asger Jorn, The Final Years: 1965-1973*, Lund Humphries, London, 1980.

Cobra (Reprint of the review): published by Jean-Michel Place (France), Van Gennep (The Netherlands), Borgen (Denmark).

FRANKENSTEIN, Alfred: *Karel Appel*. Abrams, New York, 1980. (Dutch edition, Meulenhoff/Landshoff, Amsterdam, 1980).

McLUHAN, Marshall (foreword by): *Karel Appel, Works on Paper*, Abbeville Press, New York, 1980.

CATALOGUE of the exhibition "Constant, schilderijen 1940-1980," with an introduction by J.L. Locher. Municipal Museum, The Hague, Netherlands, September 1980.

1982

CATALOGUE of the exhibition "Cobra 1948-1951," Kunstverein, Hamburg, 25 September to 7 November 1982. Introduction by Uwe Schneede.

CATALOGUE of the travelling exhibition "Cobra 1948-1951": Musée d'Art Moderne de la Ville de Paris, Paris, 9 December 1982 to 20 February 1983; Chalon-sur-Saône, 4 March to 17 April 1983; Rennes, 29 April to 12 June 1983. Articles by, among others, Sylvain Lecombre, Christian Besson and Gilles Béraud.

CATALOGUE of the exhibition "Dotremont —peintre de l'écriture—." Centre culturel de la Communauté francaise de Belgique, Wallonnie-Bruselles, Paris, 8 December-2 January 1983.

1983

LAMBERT, Jean Clarence: *Cobra un art libre*, Chêne/Hachette, Paris, 1983. Published in Dutch by Mercatorfonds, Antwerp, 1983; in English by Mercatorfonds, Antwerp, 1983 and Abbeville Press, New York, 1985; in German by Langeweische, Königstein, 1985.

1984

STOKVIS, Willemijn: "De Nederlandse bijdrage aan de Cobrabeweging en verwanten in schilder' en beeldhouwkunst," in *De Nederlandse identiteit in de kunst na 1945*, Meulenhoff/ Landshoff, Amsterdam, 1984.

CATALOGUE of the exhibition "El Movimiento Cobra en la Colección Karel van Stuijvenberg," Museo de Arte Contemporáneo de Caracas, 1984.

CATALOGUE of the exhibition "Cobra Aventures Collectives": De Zonnehof, Amersfoort, 18 September to 28 October 1984; Frans Hals Museum, Haarlem, 2 November 1984 to 6 January 1985; Kunstindustrimuseet, Copenhagen, 17 January to 17 February 1985; Nordjyllands Kunstmuseum, Aalborg, 15 March to 28 April 1985; Salle Saint-Georges, Liège, 10 May to 16 June 1985; La maison de la culture de Tournai, Kortrijk, 22 June to 10 August 1985. Articles by, among others, Gilles Béraud and Erik Slagter.

1985

APPEL, Karel: *Ceramics, sculpture, wood, reliefs, street art, murals, tapestries, villa el salvador*, with texts by Pierre Restany and Allan Ginsberg. Interview by Frédéric de Towarnicki. Abbeville Press, New York, 1985.

Documents relatifs à la fondation de l'Internationale Situationniste 1948-1957. Éditions Allia, Paris, 1985.

DOTREMONT, Christian: *Isabelle, texts on Cobra 1948-1978*, La Pierre d'Alun, Brussels, 1985.

FLOMENHAFT, Eleanor: *The roots and development of Cobra Art*. The Fine Arts Museum of Long Island (Famli), New York, 1985.

1986

BIRTWISTLE, Graham: *Asger Jorn's comprehensive theory of art between Helhesten and Cobra, 1946-1949*, Reflex, Utrecht, 1986.

CATALOGUE of the exhibition "Books and graphics of Cobra artists," organized by the Franklin Furnace Archives, City Gallery of New York City, 28 March to 26 April 1986. Organization: Richard Kempe. Introduction: Willemijn Stokvis. Ediciones Polígrafa, Barcelona / Galeria Joan Prats, New York.

CATALOGUE of the exhibition "Constant 1945-1983," with an introduction by Klaus Honnef. Rheinisches Landesmuseum, Bonn, 17 January-2 March 1986.

1987

STOKVIS, Willemijn: *Il contributo Olandese al movimento Cobra,* followed by *Il movimento Cobra nelle sue relazioni con l'Italia*, Ed. Istituto Universitario Olandese di Storia dell'Arte, Florence, Italy, 1987.

CATALOGUE of the exhibition "Asger Jorn 1914-1973," Gemälde, Zeichnungen, Aquarelle, Gouachen, Skulpturen. Editor Armin Zweite. Lenbachhaus, München, 21 January-29 March 1987.

CATALOGUE of the exhibition "Pierre Alechinsky: Margin and Center," Solomon R. Guggenheim Museum, New York, 1987.

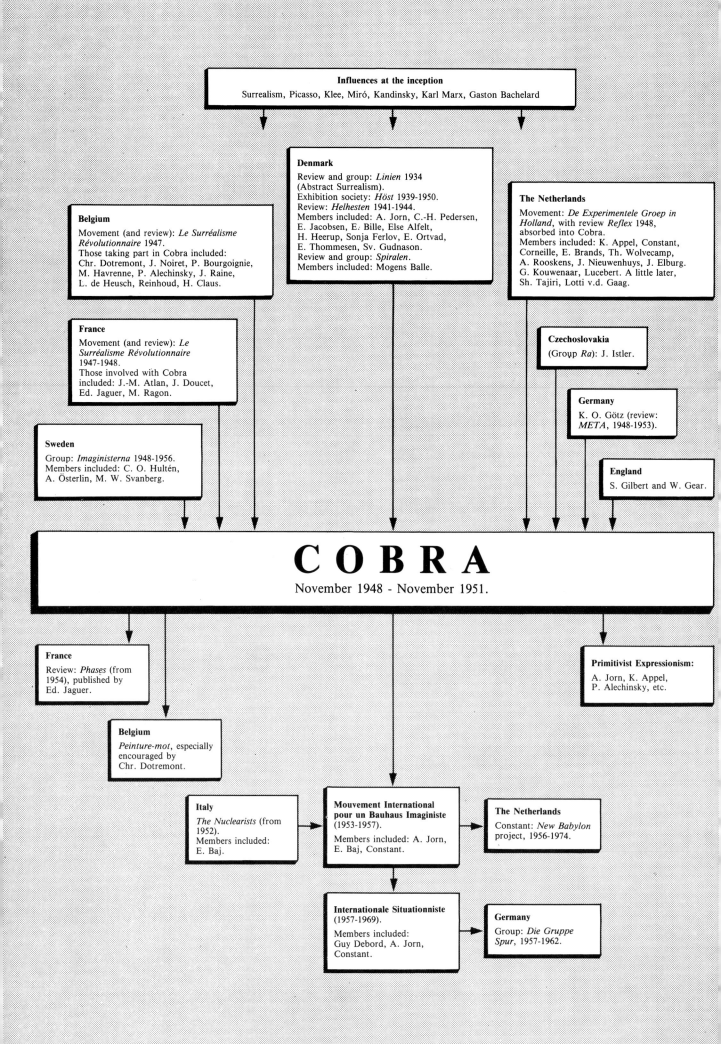

Influences at the inception
Surrealism, Picasso, Klee, Miró, Kandinsky, Karl Marx, Gaston Bachelard

Belgium
Movement (and review): *Le Surréalisme Révolutionnaire* 1947.
Those taking part in Cobra included:
Chr. Dotremont, J. Noiret, P. Bourgoignie, M. Havrenne, P. Alechinsky, J. Raine, L. de Heusch, Reinhoud, H. Claus.

Denmark
Review and group: *Linien* 1934 (Abstract Surrealism).
Exhibition society: *Höst* 1939-1950.
Review: *Helhesten* 1941-1944.
Members included: A. Jorn, C.-H. Pedersen, E. Jacobsen, E. Bille, Else Alfelt, H. Heerup, Sonja Ferlov, E. Ortvad, E. Thommesen, Sv. Gudnason.
Review and group: *Spiralen*.
Members included: Mogens Balle.

The Netherlands
Movement: *De Experimentele Groep in Holland*, with review *Reflex* 1948, absorbed into Cobra.
Members included: K. Appel, Constant, Corneille, E. Brands, Th. Wolvecamp, A. Rooskens, J. Nieuwenhuys, J. Elburg. G. Kouwenaar, Lucebert. A little later, Sh. Tajiri, Lotti v.d. Gaag.

France
Movement (and review): *Le Surréalisme Révolutionnaire* 1947-1948.
Those involved with Cobra included: J.-M. Atlan, J. Doucet, Ed. Jaguer, M. Ragon.

Czechoslovakia
(Group *Ra*): J. Istler.

Germany
K. O. Götz (review: *META*, 1948-1953).

Sweden
Group: *Imaginisterna* 1948-1956.
Members included: C. O. Hultén, A. Österlin, M. W. Svanberg.

England
S. Gilbert and W. Gear.

C O B R A
November 1948 - November 1951.

France
Review: *Phases* (from 1954), published by Ed. Jaguer.

Primitivist Expressionism:
A. Jorn, K. Appel, P. Alechinsky, etc.

Belgium
Peinture-mot, especially encouraged by Chr. Dotremont.

Italy
The Nuclearists (from 1952).
Members included: E. Baj.

Mouvement International pour un Bauhaus Imaginiste (1953-1957).
Members included: A. Jorn, E. Baj, Constant.

The Netherlands
Constant: *New Babylon* project, 1956-1974.

Internationale Situationniste (1957-1969).
Members included: Guy Debord, A. Jorn, Constant.

Germany
Group: *Die Gruppe Spur*, 1957-1962.

ILLUSTRATIONS

COLLECTIVE WORKS

1a

1b

1c

1d

2

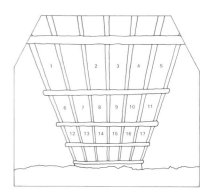

36

1a. The architects' house at Bregneröd, near Copenhagen, where the Cobra members spent the summer of 1949 (mid-August to mid-September) together and painted the interior. Everyone took part, even the children.

1b. The fireplace wall was painted by Stephen Gilbert, while Jorn moulded two arms "embracing the flames" over the fireplace itself, which was shaped like an enormous nose.

1c. In the living room (facing the fireplace), Jorn painted the left-hand wall.

1d. The right-hand wall was painted by Carl-Henning Pedersen, while the door was painted by Klaus Jorn's seven-year-old son.

2. The painted ceiling of the architects' house at Bregneröd, August/September 1949. The diagram shows the names of the artists: Anders Österlin (1-5, 14-15); Carl Otton Hultén (6, 11); Alfred H. Lilliendahl (8, 10); Asger Jorn (12); Carl-Henning Pedersen (13); Erling Jörgensen (16); Mogens Balle (17). Restored in 1969, this ceiling is now housed in the Art Society, Lyngby, Denmark.

3. Appel, Constant and Corneille painted the interior of the house of the trout farmer and potter Erik Nyholm at Funder, near Silkeborg (Denmark), in November 1949. a) In the room with the wash basin and mirror, the left-hand wall was painted by Appel, the rear wall and the furthest part of the right-hand wall by Corneille. b) The large animal figures on the right-hand wall are by Constant.
c) Constant also painted a wall and the ceiling in another room.
d) The wall to the right of this, with its door, was done by Appel. On the lintel they signed their names: Constant, Corneille, Appel, 30 November 1949.

3a

3b

3c

3d

4

4. Jorn, Appel, Constant, Corneille and Erik Nyholm painted
   over a work by Richard Mortensen a *Cobramodification*: 1949.
   Oil on canvas, 42.5 × 62.2 cm, signed above left by the three
   Dutchmen, below right by Nyholm.
   Collection Erik Nyholm, Funder, on loan to the Silkeborg Art
   Museum, Denmark.

5a. *Some of These Days*, lithograph done in Malmö (Sweden) by
    Corneille, Österlin, Appel, Constant, C.O. Hultén and Max
    Walter Svanberg. ("It was a proper Indian feast around a
    stone," Corneille said.)
    Lithograph with bistre, 40 × 39 cm, signed and dated below by
    all the artists, their names followed by "Image Press Sverige
    3/9, 25 Nov. 1949."
    Collection Karel van Stuijvenberg, Caracas.

5b. Sketch with an explanation of the lithograph (5a) by Corneille.

6. Two pages from the book *Goede morgen haan* (Good Morning,
   Rooster), with text by Gerrit Kouwenaar and drawing (coloured
   by hand) by Constant. Published in Amsterdam in 1949 as a
   publication of the "Experimentele Groep in Holland."
   17.5 × 25.2 cm, edition of 30 copies.

5a

5b

6

7

8

9

7. *Il y a plus de choses dans la terre d'un tableau que dans le ciel de la théorie esthétique* (There are more things in the earth of a picture than in the heaven of aesthetic theory).
Asger Jorn and Christian Dotremont (text).
Oil on canvas, 1947/48, 99 × 103 cm, signed by Dotremont on reverse.
Private collection, Belgium.

8. Christian Dotremont (text), Asger Jorn (drawing): two examples of the *peinture-mots* series, done between 1948 and 1953, published in Paris in 1961 under the title *La chevelure des choses*.
Ink on paper, a. 1948, 19.6 × 14.3 cm, dated below right, b. 1949, 20.5 × 14.8 cm, dated below centre.

9. Corneille (standing) and Christian Dotremont, working in Brussels in 1949 (probably in the garden of Dotremont's home in the rue de la Paille). Photograph: Henny Riemens.

10. CORNEILLE (14 gouaches, 16 × 13 cm), CHRISTIAN
DOTREMONT (14 texts): *Improvisation*, 1949.
Collection Karel van Stuijvenberg, Caracas.

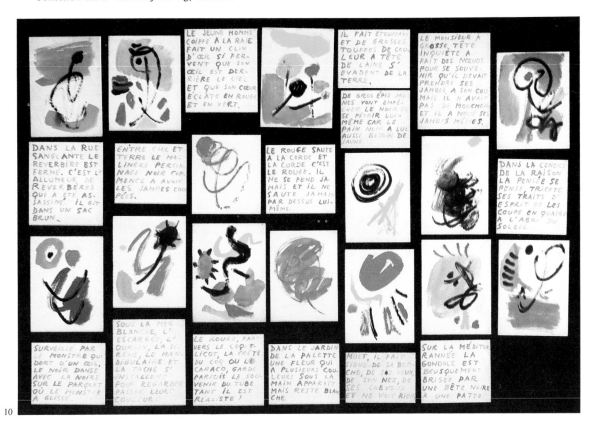

10

11

11. JEAN-MICHEL ATLAN and CHRISTIAN DOTREMONT (text):
Les transformes, 1950, a. front and back covers of a series of
six gouaches with text, each 24.1 × 35 cm. b. One of the
gouaches of the series.
Collection Karel van Stuijvenberg, Caracas.

DENMARK

Asger Jorn

12. ASGER JORN: *Untitled* (referred to as
    "Pige"), 1939.
    Oil on canvas, 61 × 61.2 cm.
    Collection Borge Venge, Aarhus, Denmark.

13. ASGER JORN: *Untitled*, 1945.
    Oil on plywood, 130 × 145 cm, signed and
    dated above left (on the reverse is a painting
    done in 1943).
    Collection J. Frost Larsen, Copenhagen.

14. ASGER JORN: *Untitled*, 1947.
    Oil on canvas, 101 × 81 cm, signed and dated
    above right.
    Collection Edouard and Simone Jaguer,
    Paris.

14

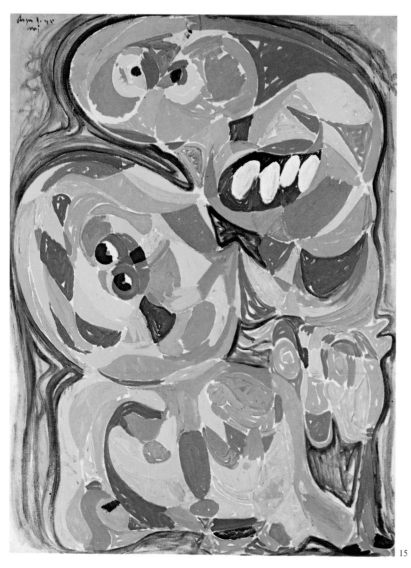

15

15. ASGER JORN: *Tolitikuja*, May 1945.
    Oil on canvas, 150×109.7 cm, signed and dated
    above left.
    Collection John Nicholas Streep, New York.
    Ref.: reproduced in *Bibliothèque de Cobra*,
    1st series, No. 14, Copenhagen, 1950.

16. ASGER JORN: *Buttadeo*, 1950.
    Oil on masonite, 90×119 cm, signed and dated
    above left on reserve.
    Collection Björn Rosengreen, Copenhagen.

17. ASGER JORN: *Midsummer Night's Dream*, 1953.
    Oil on masonite, 160.1×183 cm, signed and dated
    below centre.
    Collection Karel van Stuijvenberg, Caracas.

18. ASGER JORN: *Opus 2, af den stumme Myte*
    (On the Silent Myth, Opus 2), 1952.
    Oil on masonite, 135×300 cm, signed and dated
    on reverse.
    Municipal Library, Silkeborg, Denmark.

16

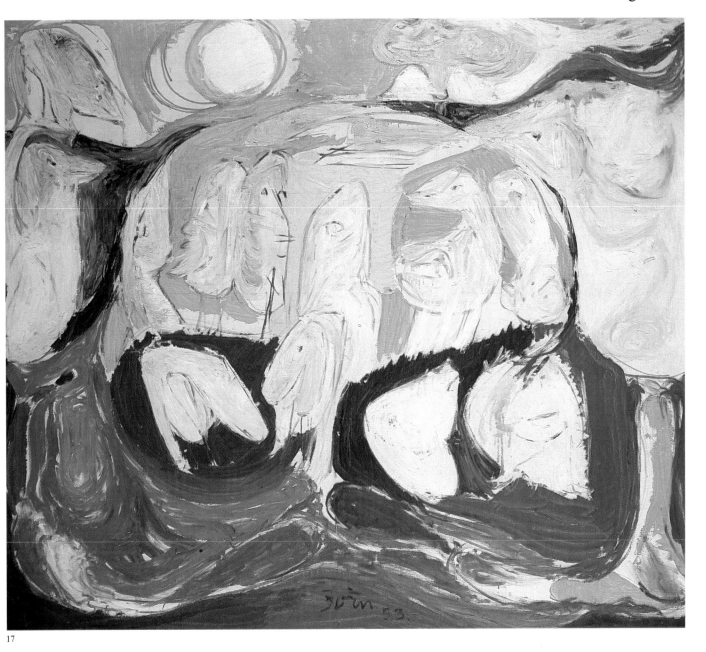

17

18

19. ASGER JORN: *Mit slot i Spanien* (My Castle in Spain), 1954.
    Oil on softboard, 122×91.5 cm, signed on reverse.
    Statens Museum for Kunst, Copenhagen.

20. ASGER JORN: *Le timide orgueilleux*, 1957.
    Oil on wood, 100×81 cm, signed and dated above right.
    Tate Gallery, London.

20

21

22

23

21. ASGER JORN: *Wiedersehen am Todesufer*, 1958.
Oil on canvas, 100×81 cm, signed below right.
Galerie Van de Loo, Munich.

22. ASGER JORN: *Le canard inquiétant*, 1959.
Oil on reused canvas (old painting modified), 53×64.5 cm,
signed and dated below right.
Silkeborg Kunstmuseum, Silkeborg, Denmark.

23. ASGER JORN: *L'Accrochage*, 1958.
Oil on canvas, 97×130 cm, signed and dated below right.
Stedelijk Van Abbemuseum, Eindhoven, Netherlands.

24

25

24. ASGER JORN: *Aarhus Mural* (complete view), 1959.
    Ceramic wall measuring about 3 × 27 m, made at the San
    Giorgio ceramic studio, Albisola, Italy, for the hall of the
    State High School, Aarhus, Denmark. Signed: San Giorgio,
    Albisola - Jorn 59.

25. ASGER JORN: *Aarhus Mural* (detail).

26. ASGER JORN: *Man in the Moon*, 1953.
    Ceramic, height 33 cm, width 25 cm, unsigned and undated.
    Silkeborg Kunstmuseum, Silkeborg, Denmark.

27. ASGER JORN: *Hors d'âge*, 1972.
    Oil on canvas, 150 × 195 cm, signed below right.
    Collection Marion Lefebre Burge, New York.

26

27

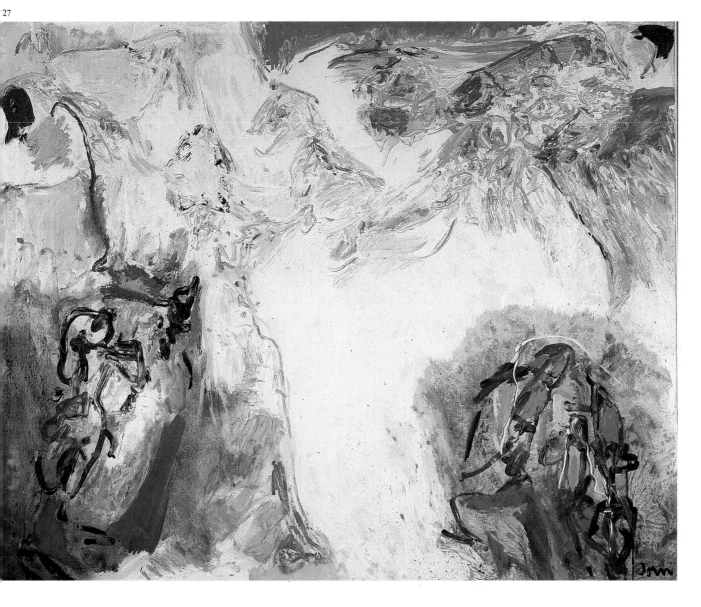

28

29

30

28. CARL-HENNING PEDERSEN: *Röd hest* (Red Horse), 1941.
Watercolour and chalk on paper, 43×50 cm, signed and dated below left.
Nordjyllands Kunstmuseum, Aalborg, Denmark.

29. CARL-HENNING PEDERSEN: *Den aedende* (The Glutton), 1939.
Oil on canvas, 100×130 cm, unsigned.
Nordjyllands Kunstmuseum, Aalborg, Denmark.
Ref.: reproduced in the *Bibliothèque de Cobra*, 1st series, No. 14,
Copenhagen, 1950.

30. CARL-HENNING PEDERSEN: *Lyseröd sol* (Light Red Sun), 1942.
Oil on canvas, 96×96 cm, signed and dated on reverse.
Carl-Henning Pedersen og Else Alfelts Museum, Herning, Denmark.

31. CARL-HENNING PEDERSEN: *Legen om det gyldne trae*
(Play round the Golden Tree), 1948.
Oil on canvas, 98 × 122 cm, signed and dated on reverse.
Carl-Henning Pedersen og Else Alfelts Museum, Herning,
Denmark.

31

32. CARL-HENNING PEDERSEN: *Staaende orange figurer* (Standing Orange Figures), 1949.
    Oil on canvas, 122 × 103 cm, unsigned and undated.
    Nordjyllands Kunstmuseum, Aalborg, Denmark.
    Ref.: reproduced in *Cobra*, No. 5, Hanover, 1950.

33. CARL-HENNING PEDERSEN: *Stjernehoveder* (Starheads), 1950.
    Oil on canvas, 101.5 × 122 cm, signed and dated on reverse.
    Louisiana Museum, Humlebaek, Denmark.

32

33

34. CARL-HENNING PEDERSEN: *Stjernehest over by* (Starhorse over the Town), 1953.
Indian ink on paper, 41×30 cm, signed and dated below left.

35. CARL-HENNING PEDERSEN: *Den leende* (The Laughing One), 1953.
Indian ink on paper, 41×30 cm, signed and dated below right.

36. CARL-HENNING PEDERSEN: *Legende om menneske og havet* (Legends about People and the Sea), 1957.
Oil on canvas mounted on masonite, 243×400 cm, unsigned and undated.
Louisiana Museum, Humlebaek, Denmark. (This work won the Guggenheim International Award for Denmark in 1958.)

34

35

36

37. CARL-HENNING PEDERSEN: *Himmelflugten* (Flight in Heaven), 1967.
Oil on canvas, 122 × 103 cm, signed and dated on reverse.
Carl-Henning Pedersen og Else Alfelts Museum, Herning, Denmark.

37

38

39

38. EGILL JACOBSEN: *Obhobning* (Pile-up), 1938-39.
Oil on canvas, 80 × 65.5 cm, signed on reverse.
Statens Museum for Kunst, Copenhagen.
Ref.: reproduced in *Cobra*, No. 4, Amsterdam,
November 1949, and in *Bibliothèque de Cobra*,
1st series, No. 13, Copenhagen, 1950.

39. EGILL JACOBSEN: *Orange objekt* (Orange Object),
1940.
Oil on canvas, 130 × 90.5 cm, signed and dated on
reverse.
Statens Museum for Kunst, Copenhagen.
Ref.: reproduced in *Cobra*, No. 4, Amsterdam,
November 1949, and in *Bibliothèque de Cobra*,
1st series, No. 13, Copenhagen, 1950.

40. EGILL JACOBSEN: *Fuglemenneske* (Birdman), 1943.
Oil on canvas, 130 × 90 cm, signed on reverse.
Collection Einar Madsen, Silkeborg, Denmark.

40

DENMARK / Egill Jacobsen

41

42

43

44

41. EGILL JACOBSEN: *Graeshoppedans* (Dance of the Grasshoppers), 1941.
Oil on canvas, 90×115 cm, signed and dated on reverse.
Nordjyllands Kunstmuseum, Aalborg, Denmark.

42. EGILL JACOBSEN: *Maske* (Mask), 1947.
Oil on canvas, 100×76 cm, unsigned and undated.
Nordjyllands Kunstmuseum, Aalborg, Denmark.

43. EJLER BILLE: *Ögle* (Lizard), 1936.
Artificial stone, height 16.5 cm (about five produced).
Statensmuseum for Kunst, Copenhagen.

44. EJLER BILLE: *Figuerer i magisk landskap - Komposition i brunt* (Figures in a Magic Landscape - Composition in Brown), 1939.
Oil on canvas, 91×65 cm, signed and dated on reverse.
Nordjyllands Kunstmuseum, Aalborg, Denmark.
Ref.: reproduced in *Bibliothèque de Cobra*, 1st series, No. 5, Copenhagen, 1950.

45

45. EJLER BILLE: *Figur Komposition i grönt* (Figure Composition in Green), 1947. Oil on canvas, 102 × 97 cm, signed and dated on reverse. Statensmuseum for Kunst, Copenhagen. Ref.: reproduced in *Bibliothèque de Cobra*, 1st series, No. 5, Copenhagen, 1950.

46. EJLER BILLE: *Forskellige figurer* (Various Figures), 1941. Oil on canvas, 91 × 65 cm, signed and dated on reverse. Nordjyllands Kunstmuseum, Aalborg, Denmark.

47. EJLER BILLE: *Figurer omkring rödt* (Figures around Red), Mönge 1953. Oil on canvas, 63.5 × 80.5 cm, signed and dated on reverse. Statensmuseum for Kunst, Copenhagen.

46

47

48. HENRY HEERUP: *Kone med barnevogn*
    (Woman with Pram), 1935.
    Alabaster, height 19 cm.
    Collection Esther Nielsen, Copenhagen.

49. HENRY HEERUP: *Landscape near Stensbij*, 1936.
    Oil on canvas, 100×86 cm, signed below right, dated below left.
    Galerie Nova Spectra, The Hague, Netherlands.

50. HENRY HEERUP: *Grammofonmanden*
    (The Gramophone Man), 1935.
    Painted wood and iron, height 178 cm.
    Nordjyllands Kunstmuseum, Aalborg, Denmark.

48

1936   HEERUP
49

50

51. HENRY HEERUP: *Glad barn* (Happy Child), 1941.
Soapstone, height 40 cm.
Formerly Collection Elise Johansen, Copenhagen.

52. HENRY HEERUP: *Relief*, ca. 1937.
Waste material, height 46 cm.
Private collection, Copenhagen.

53. HENRY HEERUP: *Billeddrejer* (Peepshow), 1940.
Wood and oil on canvas, height 77 cm.
Galerie Nova Spectra, The Hague, Netherlands.

54. HENRY HEERUP: *Dödenhöster* (Harvester of Death), 1943.
Waste material, height 75 cm.
Louisiana Museum, Humlebaek, Denmark.

51

53

52

54

55

56

57

55. HENRY HEERUP: *Cyclist with Nude*, 1940.
Oil on canvas, 80.5 × 110 cm, signed and dated below left.
Nordjyllands Kunstmuseum, Aalborg, Denmark.

56. HENRY HEERUP: *Child in Wheelbarrow*, 1944.
Oil on canvas, 45 × 65 cm, signed and dated below right.
Galerie Nova Spectra, The Hague, Netherlands.

57. HENRY HEERUP: *Gorillaen* (The Gorilla), 1943.
Granite, partly painted, ca. 105 × 97 cm.
Collection Prof. Erik Andreasen, Lyngby, near Copenhagen.

58

58. ELSE ALFELT: *Spidser der raekker mod himmlen*
(Mountaintops Reaching Towards Heaven), 1945.
Oil on panel, 127 × 127 cm, unsigned.
Carl-Henning Pedersens og Else Alfelts Museum, Herning, Denmark.
Ref.: reproduced in *Bibliothèque de Cobra*, 1st series, No. 2, Copenhagen, 1950.

59. ELSE ALFELT: *Fjellet II* (Rock II), 1945.
Oil on cardboard, 70 × 100 cm, signed and dated on reverse.
Carl-Henning Pedersens og Else Alfelts Museum, Herning, Denmark.
Ref.: reproduced in *Bibliothèque de Cobra*, 1st series, No. 2, Copenhagen, 1950.

59

60

61

60. SONJA FERLOV: *Skulptur*, 1939.
Plaster, height 36 cm, signed below left.
Collection Ole Stockmar, Denmark.
Ref.: reproduced in *Bibliothèque de Cobra*, 1st series, No. 9, Copenhagen, 1950.

61. SONJA FERLOV: *Skulptur*, 1949.
Bronze (originally plaster), height 28 cm.
Louisiana Museum, Humlebaek, Denmark.
Ref.: reproduced in *Bibliothèque de Cobra*, 1st series, No. 9, Copenhagen, 1950.

DENMARK / Erik Thommesen • Erik Ortvad

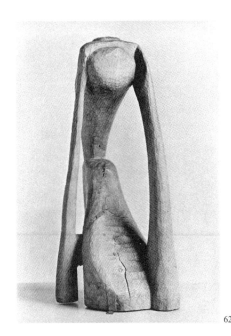

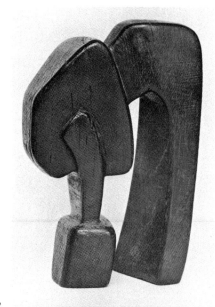

62

63

64

70

62. ERIK THOMMESEN: *Kvindebuste med fletninger*
(Bust of Woman with Plaits). 1941.
Ash, height 53 cm.
Statensmuseum for Kunst, Copenhagen.

63. ERIK THOMMESEN: *Mand* (Man), 1948.
Bog oak, height 17 cm.
Collection Ole Schierbeck, Copenhagen.

64. ERIK ORTVAD: *People and Horses*, Moräng 1944.
Oil on canvas mounted on masonite, 80 × 100 cm, signed and
dated on reverse.
Galerie Espace, Amsterdam.

65. MOGENS BALLE: *Untitled*, 1951.
Oil on canvas, 144 × 98 cm, signed below right.
Collection Sam and Ruth Kaner, Copenhagen.

66. SVAVAR GUDNASON: *Sankt Hans Dröm* (St John's Dream or
Midsummer Dream), 1941.
Oil on canvas, 97.5 × 130 cm.
Nordjyllands Kunstmuseum, Aalborg, Denmark.
Ref.: reproduced in *Helhesten*, 1st series, No. 5/6, and in
Bibliothèque de Cobra, 1st series, No. 11, Copenhagen, 1950.

65

66

71

THE NETHERLANDS

Karel Appel

67

67. KAREL APPEL: *Orgeldraaier* (Organ Grinder), 1947.
Gouache and pastel on paper, 43.8 × 55.7 cm, signed and dated below right.
Stedelijk Museum, Schiedam, Netherlands.

68. KAREL APPEL: *Vrijheidsschreeuw* (Cry for Freedom), 1948.
Oil on canvas, 100 × 79 cm, signed and dated below left.
Collection Bijko, Amsterdam.
Ref.: reproduced in *Bibliothèque de Cobra*, 1st series, No. 3,
Copenhagen, 1950.

69. KAREL APPEL: *Vragende Kinderen* (Questioning Children), 1949.
Wooden relief, painted in oils, 87 × 60 cm, signed and dated
below right.
Property of the artist.

70. KAREL APPEL: *Hiep, hiep, hoera!*, 1949.
Oil on canvas, 82 × 129 cm, signed and dated below right.
Property of the artist, on loan to the Tate Gallery, London.

72

68

69

70

71

72

73

71. KAREL APPEL: *Jongetje op speelgoedpaard*
(Boy on a Hobbyhorse), 1949.
Oil on canvas, 73 × 65 cm, signed and dated above left.
Private collection, Italy.

72. KAREL APPEL: *Vragende Kinderen* (Questioning Children), 1949.
Mural painting in the canteen of the (former) Town Hall of
Amsterdam, Waterglass paint on cement-sand mixture,
281 × 396 cm, signed and dated below left.
(Owing to the fact that the Town Hall officials disliked the
painting, it was covered over with wallpaper and remained
hidden from view for ten years.)

73. KAREL APPEL: *De ontmoeting* (The Meeting), 1951.
Oil on canvas, 130 × 97.5 cm, signed and dated below left.
Collection Rijkdienst Beeldende Kunst, The Hague,
Netherlands, on loan to the Centraal Museum, Utrecht.

THE NETHERLANDS / Karel Appel

74

75

74. KAREL APPEL: *De dolle verhuizing* (The Crazy Move), 1951.
    Gouache, chalk and pencil on paper, cut out and stuck on
    wrapping paper, ca. 155 × 101 cm, signed and dated below left.
    Property of the artist.

75 KAREL APPEL: *Mens* (Human Being), 1953.
    Oil on canvas, 210 × 130 cm, signed and dated below right.
    Stedelijk Museum, Amsterdam.

76. KAREL APPEL: *Portrait of Willem Sandberg*, 1956.
    Oil on canvas, 130 × 90 cm, signed and dated below right.
    Collection Mr Power, London.

77

77. KAREL APPEL: *Barbaars naakt* (Barbaric Nude), 1957.
Oil on canvas, 130×190 cm, signed and dated below left.
Museum van Hedendaagse Kunst, Ghent, Belgium.

78. KAREL APPEL: *Feest in Lapland* (Feast in Lapland), 1958.
Oil on canvas, signed and dated below right.
Stedelijk Museum, Amsterdam.

79. KAREL APPEL: *From the Beginning*, 1961.
Oil on canvas, 230×300 cm, signed and dated below right.
Stedelijk Museum, Amsterdam.

78

79

80

81

80. CONSTANT: *Twee dieren* (Two Animals),
    1946.
    Oil on canvas, 60×65 cm, signed and
    dated below right.
    Collection De Jong, Ascona, Switzerland.

81. CONSTANT: *Het laddertje*
    (The Little Ladder), 1949.
    Oil on canvas, 90×75 cm, signed and
    dated below right.
    Gemeente Museum, The Hague,
    Netherlands.

82. CONSTANT: *Fauna*, 1949.
    Oil on canvas, 70×85 cm, signed and
    dated below left.
    Collection De Jong, Ascona, Switzerland.
    Ref.: reproduced in *Bibliothèque de
    Cobra*, 1st series, No. 6, Copenhagen,
    1950.

83. CONSTANT: *Fête de la tristesse*, 1949.
    Oil on canvas, 85×110 cm, signed and
    dated above centre.
    Collection Rijksdienst Beeldende Kunst,
    The Hague, Netherlands, on loan to the
    Museum Boymans/Van Beuningen,
    Rotterdam.

82

83

84. CONSTANT: *De oorlog* (The War), 1950.
    Oil on canvas, 126×117 cm, signed and dated below left.
    Stedelijk Van Abbe Museum, Eindhoven, Netherlands.

85. CONSTANT: *Verschroeide aarde I* (Scorched Earth I), 1951.
    Oil on canvas, 145×111 cm, signed and dated below right.
    Stedelijk Museum, Amsterdam.

84

85

86

86. CONSTANT: *Homo Ludens*, 1964.
Oil on canvas, 160×185 cm, signed and dated below left.
Stedelijk Museum, Amsterdam.

87. CONSTANT: Models of sections of the city of the future *New Babylon:*
a. *Construction in Orange*, 1958.
Metal, perspex, wood, 110×110×24 cm;
b. *Space-furrow with base plate - concert hall for electronic music*, 1960.
Metal, perspex, wood, 65 × (base plate) 90×65 cm;
c. *Ladder-Labyrinth*, 1967.
Brass, perspex, wood, 97×86×76 cm,
Wilhelm Lehmbruck Museum, Duisburg, West Germany.

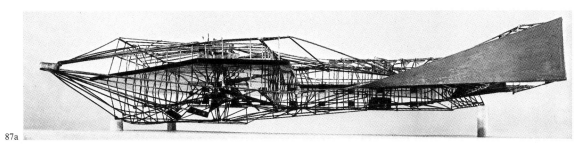

87a

b

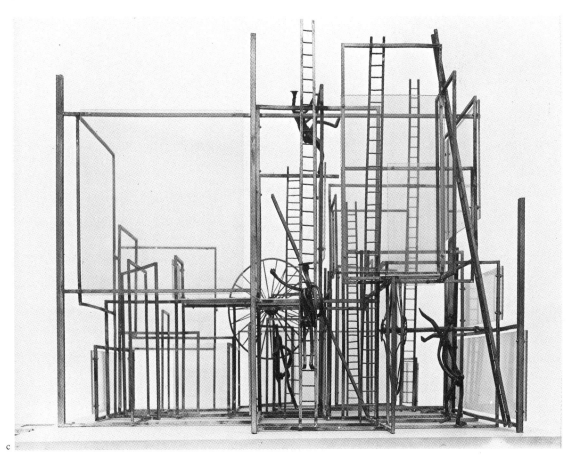

c

88

88. CONSTANT: *Le Massacre*, 1972.
 Oil on canvas, 120×130 cm, signed and dated below left.
 Private collection.

89. CONSTANT: *De ontmoeting tussen Ubu en Justine*
 (The Meeting of Ubu and Justine), 1975.
 Oil on canvas, 190×200 cm, signed and dated centre right.
 Stedelijk Museum, Amsterdam.

90. CONSTANT: *L'Interrogatoire*, 1983.
 Oil on canvas, 131×141 cm, signed and dated below right.
 Property of the artist.

89

90

91

92

91. CORNEILLE: *Vogels* (Birds), 1948.
Gouache on paper, 113 × 138 cm, signed and dated
below left.
Collection Karel van Stuijvenberg, Caracas, on loan
to the Stedelijk Museum, Amsterdam.

92. CORNEILLE: *Le port en tête*, 1949.
Watercolour, ink, collage and newsprint on paper,
48.2 × 37 cm, signed and dated below centre.
Stedelijk Museum, Schiedam, Netherlands.
Ref.: reproduced in *Bibliothèque de Cobra*,
1st series, No. 7, Copenhagen, 1950.

93. CORNEILLE: *Le retour du marin*, 1949.
Oil on canvas, 70 × 50 cm, signed and dated below
centre.
Collection E. Kuijper-Sluijters, Amsterdam.
Ref.: reproduced in *Bibliothèque de Cobra*,
1st series, No. 7, Copenhagen, 1950.

94

94. CORNEILLE: *Le rythme joyeux de la ville*, 1949.
Oil on canvas, 58.5 × 49 cm, signed and dated below right.
Stedelijk Museum, Amsterdam.
Ref.: reproduced in *Cobra*, No. 4, Amsterdam, 1949.

95. CORNEILLE: *Village indigène*, 1951.
Oil on canvas, 65 × 90 cm, signed and dated above left.
Private collection, Paris.
Ref.: reproduced in *Cobra*, No. 10, Liège, 1951.

96. CORNEILLE: *Vis* (Fish), 1950.
Watercolour on paper, 38.6 × 50.3 cm, signed and dated above right.
Stedelijk Museum, Schiedam, Netherlands.

97. CORNEILLE: *Pierres et fleurs*, 1955.
Oil on canvas, 53 × 76 cm, signed and dated above left.
Stedelijk Museum, Schiedam, Netherlands.

95

96

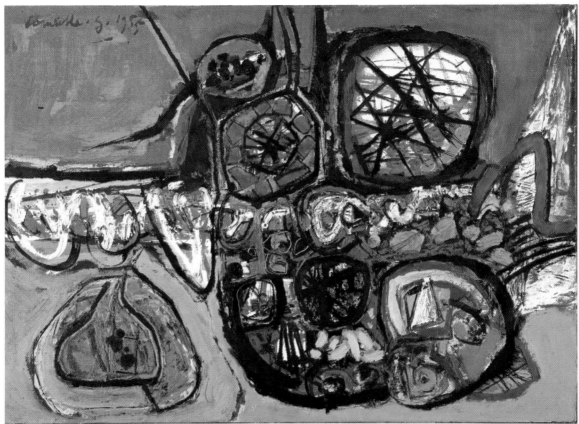

97

98

98. CORNEILLE: *Le port blanc* or *Heure matinale*, 1956.
Oil on canvas, 64.7 × 53.5 cm, signed and dated below right.
Stedelijk Museum, Schiedam, Netherlands.

99. CORNEILLE: *Dans un jardin avec des oiseaux*, 1962.
Oil on canvas, 89 × 116 cm, signed and dated below centre.
Stedelijk Museum, Amsterdam.

100. CORNEILLE: *Terre pastorale*, 1966.
Oil on canvas, 162 × 130 cm, signed and dated below right.
Stedelijk Museum, Amsterdam.

99

100

101. CORNEILLE: *Palmier-roi*, 1972.
     Acrylic on canvas, 162 × 130 cm, signed and dated below centre.

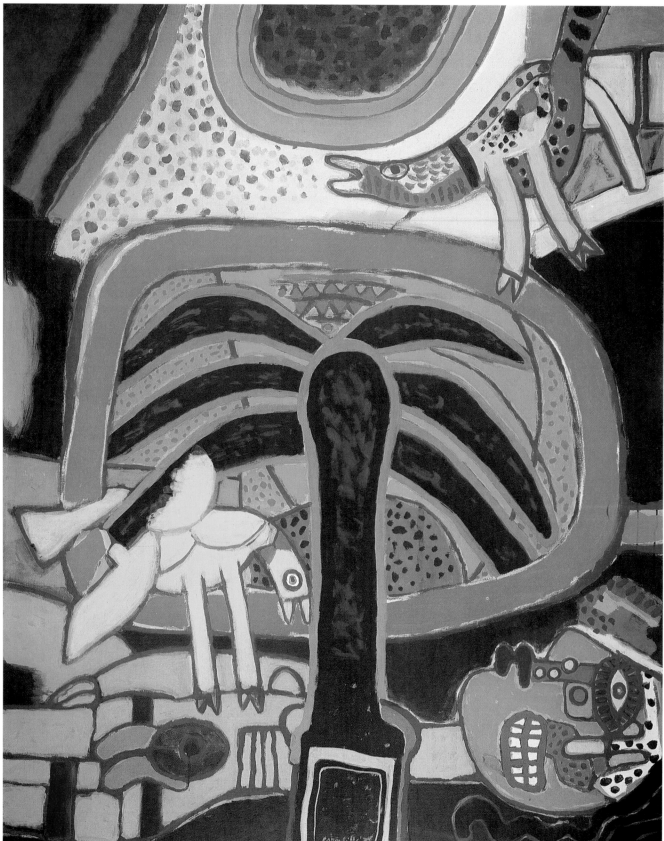

101

102. ANTON ROOSKENS: *Composition*, undated (ca. 1950).
 Oil on canvas, 94 × 104.8 cm, signed below right and on reverse.
 Stedelijk Museum, Schiedam, Netherlands.

102

103

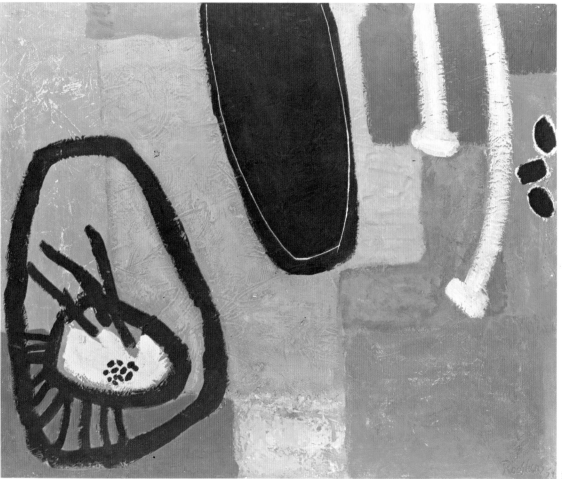

104

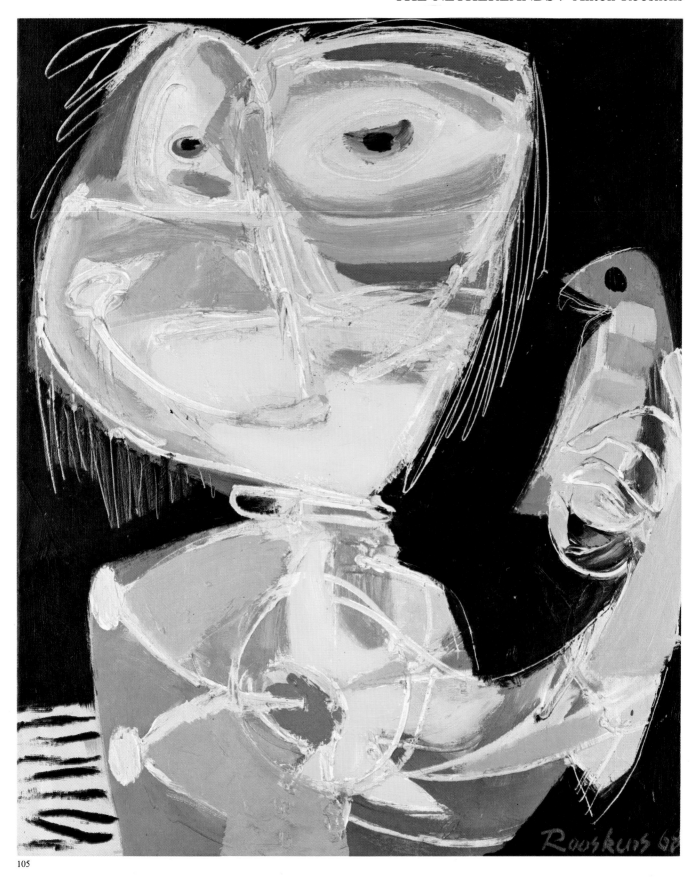

105

103. ANTON ROOSKENS: *Composition*, 1952.
Oil on canvas, 95 × 114.5 cm, signed and dated below right.
Stedelijk Museum, Schiedam, Netherlands.

104. ANTON ROOSKENS: *African Forms*, 1954.
Oil on canvas, 100 × 122 cm, signed and dated below right.
Stedelijk Museum, Amsterdam.

105. ANTON ROOSKENS: *Vrouw met vogel* (Woman with Bird), 1968.
Oil on canvas, 80 × 65 cm, signed and dated below right.
Collection Sam and Ruth Kaner, Copenhagen.

106

107

08

06. THEO WOLVECAMP: *Explosion*, 1948.
    Oil on canvas, 70×80 cm, signed and dated above right.
    Stedelijk Museum, Amsterdam.

07. JAN NIEUWENHUYS: *Slaapwandelende haan* (Sleepwalking Rooster), ca. 1949.
    Oil, cardboard, collage on canvas, 69.8×99.8 cm, signed below right.
    Stedelijk Museum, Schiedam, Netherlands.

08. THEO WOLVECAMP: *Composition B3*, 1949.
    Oil on canvas, 90×80.5 cm, signed below right.
    Stedelijk Museum, Amsterdam.
    Ref.: reproduced in *Cobra*, No. 5, Hanover, 1950.

109

109. THEO WOLVECAMP: *Tauromachie*, 1957.
   Oil on canvas, 110×110 cm, signed below centre and on reverse.
   Private collection.

110. EUGÈNE BRANDS: *Two Shapes*, 1949.
   Oil on canvas, 69.5×109.5 cm, signed and dated below left.
   Collection Rijksdienst Beeldende Kunst, The Hague, Netherlands, on loan to the
   Stedelijk Museum, Schiedam, Netherlands.

111. EUGÈNE BRANDS: *De vrouw van de horlogemaker* (The Watchmaker's Wife), 1952.
   Oil on canvas, 100.5×95.5 cm, signed and dated above right.
   Collection Sylvia and Jerry Cohn, Nebraska, U.S.A.

110

111

112. EUGÈNE BRANDS: *The Black Tower* or *Activité magique*, 3/1951.
  Oil on canvas, 106×103 cm, signed and dated below left.
  Collection S.T. Boen, Netherlands.

112

113. EUGÈNE BRANDS:
Small Black Moon, 1949.
Waste material on wooden
panel, 48 × 53 cm,
signed and dated below right.
Collection Geer Hofland,
Heemstede, Netherlands.

114. EUGÈNE BRANDS:
Dynamic Landscape, 1976.
Oil on canvas, 200 × 235 cm,
signed and dated below right.
Galerie Mia Joosten,
Amsterdam.

113

114

103

THE NETHERLANDS / Lucebert

115. LUCEBERT: *Orpheus and the Animals*, 1952.
   Gouache, ink and coloured pencils on paper, 41.8 × 56.4 cm,
   signed and dated below centre.
   Stedelijk Museum, Amsterdam.

116. LUCEBERT: *Voel de tijd aan de tand* (The Teeth of the Evidence), 1952.
   Gouache and collage on paper, 41 × 51 cm, unsigned.
   Collection Peter Selinka, Ravensburg, Germany.

115

116

117

117. LUCEBERT: *Spanish Dance*, 1961.
Oil on canvas, 185 × 134.5 cm,
signed and dated below left.
Collection Evert van Tright,
Middelrode, Netherlands.

118. LUCEBERT: *Two Heads*, 1962.
Oil on canvas, 90 × 120 cm, signed
and dated.
Private collection.

118

119. LUCEBERT: *The Prisoner*, 1964.
Oil on canvas, 130×90 cm, signed and dated below right.
Stedelijk Museum, Amsterdam.

120. LOTTI VAN DER GAAG: *The Waiting*, 1951.
Terracotta (once cast in bronze), 62 × 51 × 36.5 cm, signed on the foot.
Museum Boymans/Van Beuningen, Rotterdam, Netherlands (bronze).

121. SHINKICHI TAJIRI: *Eendagssculpturen aan de Seine* (One-day
Sculptures on the Seine), 1952.
Scrap metal (destroyed).
Photograph: Sabine Weiss.

120

121

BELGIUM

Pierre Alechinsky

122

122. PIERRE ALECHINSKY: *Exercice de nuit*, 1950.
Gouache on paper, 58 × 51 cm, signed and
dated below left.
Collection Stéphane Janssen, Beverly Hills,
California, U.S.A.

123. PIERRE ALECHINSKY: Three of a series of
nine etchings entitled *Les Métiers*, 1948.
a. *Le bûcheron*; b. *Le soldat*; c. *Le coiffeur*.
Each about 13.5 × 10 cm.
The accompanying texts were written by Luc
Zangrie (Luc de Heusch),

124. PIERRE ALECHINSKY: *Les mers intérieurs*,
June 1958.
Oil on canvas, 200 × 200 cm, signed below right,
dated on reverse.
Galerie Nova Spectra, The Hague, Netherlands.

123a

b

c

124

125

126

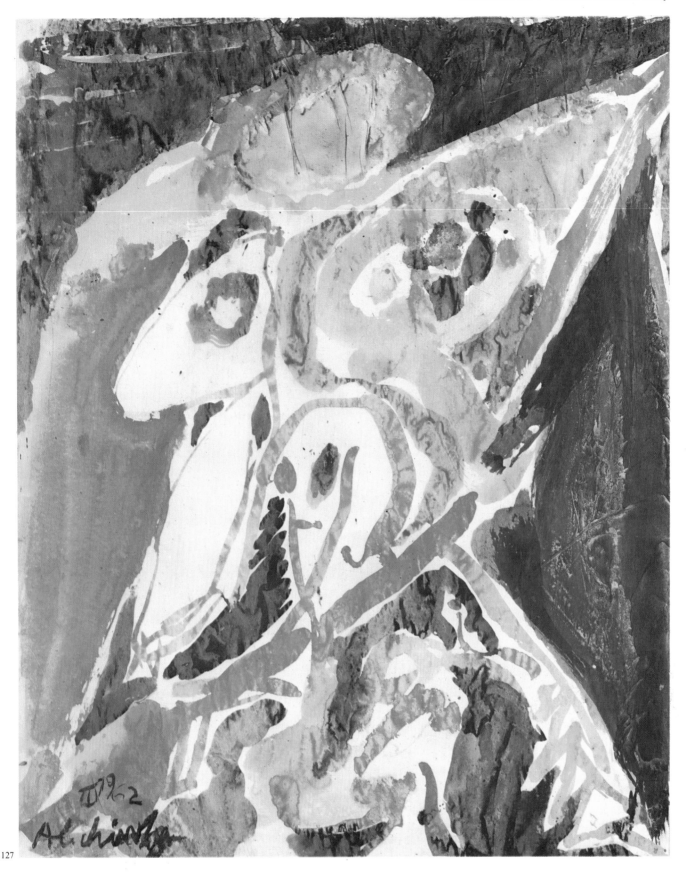

127

125. PIERRE ALECHINSKY: *Les polyglottes*, 1960.
Indian ink and tempera on paper, glued on wood and finished
with resin, 100 × 150 cm, signed and dated below right.
Collection André Nagar, Paris.

126. PIERRE ALECHINSKY: *Alice grandit*, 1961.
Oil on canvas, 205 × 245 cm, signed and dated below right.
Private collection.

127. PIERRE ALECHINSKY: *Dragon terrassant le petit Michel*, 1962.
Watercolour on paper, glued on canvas and finished with
resin, 90 × 90 cm, signed and dated below left.
Collection Mr and Mrs Raymond Haas, Paris.

111

128. PIERRE ALECHINSKY: *La jeune fille et la Mort*, 1967.
Acrylic and Indian ink on paper, glued on canvas,
137 × 137 cm, signed and dated below right.
Collection Marion Lefebre Burge, New York.

129. PIERRE ALECHINSKY: *L'Absent entouré*, 1973.
Acrylic on paper, glued on canvas, 114 × 154 cm, signed and
dated below right.

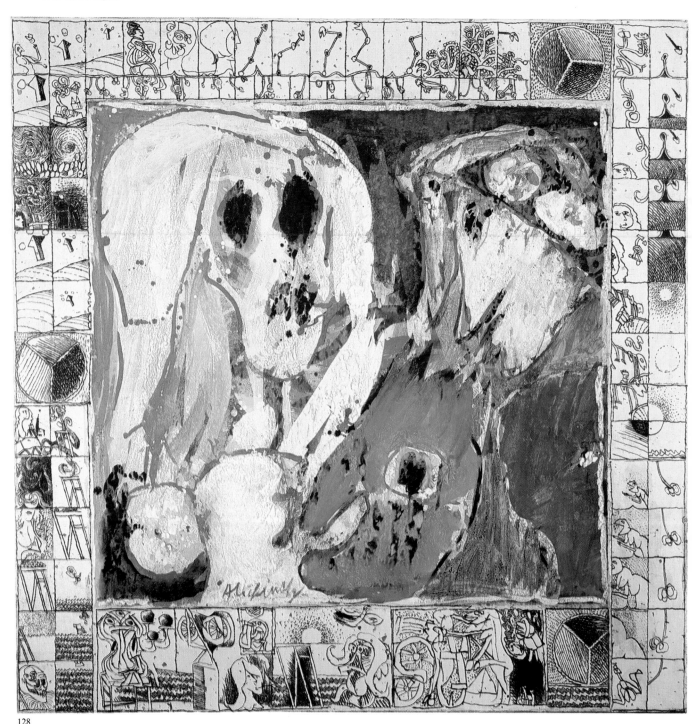

128

130. PIERRE ALECHINSKY: *Cordelière* (The Franciscan Nun), 1973.
  Acrylic on paper, glued on canvas (with predella), 184 × 153 cm,
  signed below left.
  Collection Karel van Stuijvenberg, Caracas.

130

132

131

131. CHRISTIAN DOTREMONT: *si désolé que soit dans l'Extrême-Nord l'hiver et si sombre que soit la nuit que nous venions ajouter encore à cette nuit, nous y trouvions énormément de luminosités, moins dans les éclats du ciel, réel, proche, ou de la terre infiniment neigeuse, ou d'une brusque aurore boréale, que dans la sensation probablement indéfinissable de vivre tout ce que nous voyions et plus*, 1974.
Indian ink on paper, 67 × 134 cm, unsigned and undated.

132. CHRISTIAN DOTREMONT: *poudreux patatras de printemps*, 1969.
Indian ink on paper, 72 × 54 cm, unsigned and undated.

133. CHRISTIAN DOTREMONT (text) and MOGENS BALLE (painting):
Une peinture doit être ouverte et un peu fermée, 1962.
Oil on canvas, 72×92 cm, signed below left M.B.
Collection Mogens Balle, Kalundborg, Denmark.

134. JAN COX: *"Ne fait pas le vilain..."*.
Lithograph, 30×23 cm, signed below right.
Ref.: published in *Cobra*, No. 6, Brussels, April 1950.

135. HUGO CLAUS: *Delstof*.
Poem illustrated by the author himself, published in *Cobra*, No. 6, Brussels, April 1950.

133

134

135

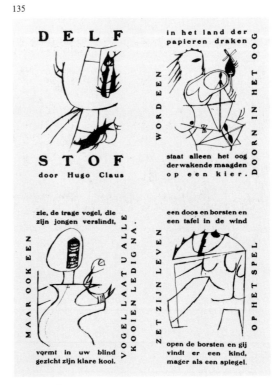

136. CHRISTIAN DOTREMONT (calligraphy on predella, in Indian ink), PIERRE ALECHINSKY (acrylic):
"Ondes extrêmes du feu du fond d'une Ande grimpé de bondissements par une corde granitique de strates Ondes dansantes du choc de fond des âges fondus en feu jusqu'à fendre en lèvres les neiges les terres pour verser le cri Ondes hurleuses mais chanteuses du choc porteuses de danger chanteuses vers l'aube glissées de l'aubier comme les feuilles premières ou dernières d'un arbre sur le ciel atteint de terre."
On paper, 151 × 154 cm, glued on canvas, signed and dated below left in acrylic by Alechinsky, and below right in ink by Dotremont. 1974-79. Collection Pierre Alechinsky, Bougival, France.

136

137. REINHOUD: *Alien*, 1958.
     Copper, 200 × 160 × 97 cm.
     Museum van Hedendaagse Kunst, Ghent, Belgium.

138. REINHOUD: *Les baladins*, 1972.
     Copper, now toghether mounted on one socle, and 45 × 48 × 27 cm.
     Private collection, Denmark.

137

138

FRANCE

Jean-Michel Atlan

139

140

139. JEAN-MICHEL ATLAN: *Samba zapotèque*,
    1957.
    Oil on canvas, 116×73 cm, signed and dated
    below left.
    Private collection.

140. JEAN-MICHEL ATLAN: *Untitled*, ca. 1947.
    Oil on canvas, 100×81 cm, signed below right.
    Galerie Nova Spectra, The Hague, Netherlands.

141

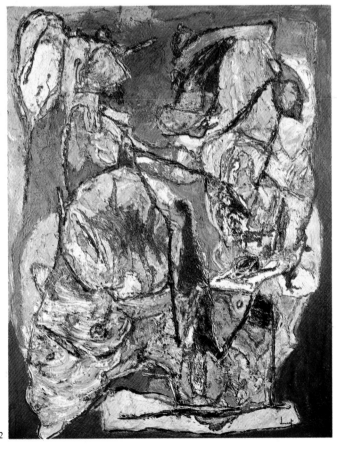

141. JACQUES DOUCET: *Untitled*, 1949.
     Watercolour on paper, 32 × 48 cm, signed and dated
     below right.
     Galerie Nova Spectra, The Hague, Netherlands.

142. JACQUES DOUCET: *Le dialogue de l'Egée*, 1978-81.
     Oil on canvas, 146 × 114 cm, signed below right.
     Private collection, Belgium.

142

ENGLAND

Stephen Gilbert

143

143. STEPHEN GILBERT: *Mariposa*, 1948.
   Oil on canvas, 41×51 cm, signed and dated below right.
   Collection Karel van Stuijvenberg, Caracas.

144. WILLIAM GEAR: *Celtic Composition*, 1948.
   Oil on canvas, 54×73 cm, signed and dated below right.
   Collection Karel van Stuijvenberg, Caracas.

145. KARL OTTO GÖTZ: *Nightmare*, 1948.
   Monotype, 44.7×63 cm.
   Property of the artist.

144

145

SWEDEN

Carl Otto Hultén • Anders Österlin

146

147

148

146. CARL OTTO HULTÉN: *Stadens kvinna kysser* (City Woman Kissing), 1951.
Oil on canvas, 82.5 × 131 cm, signed above right.
Malmö Konstmuseet, Malmö, Sweden.

147. ANDERS ÖSTERLIN: *Imaginar röd* (Imaginary Red), 1950.
Oil on canvas, 60.7 × 68.2 cm, signed and dated below right.
Malmö Konstmuseet, Malmö, Sweden.

148. MAX WALTER SVANBERG: *Imagination*, 1949.
Wax, tempera and ink on paper, 37 × 44.5 cm, signed and dated below centre.
Malmö Konstmuseet, Malmö, Sweden.

List of illustrations

80. CONSTANT: *Two Animals*, 1946, oil on canvas.

81. CONSTANT: *The Little Ladder*, 1949, oil on canvas.

82. CONSTANT: *Fauna*, 1949, oil on canvas.

83. CONSTANT: *Fête de la tristesse*, 1949, oil on canvas.

84. CONSTANT: *The War*, 1950, oil on canvas.

85. CONSTANT: *Scorched Earth I*, 1951, oil on canvas.

86. CONSTANT: *Homo Ludens*, 1964, oil on canvas.

87. CONSTANT: Models for *New Babylon*, a. 1958; b. 1960; c. 1967.

88. CONSTANT: *Le Massacre*, 1972, oil on canvas.

89. CONSTANT: *The Meeting of Ubu and Justine*, 1975, oil on canvas.

90. CONSTANT: *L'Interrogatoire*, 1983, oil on canvas.

91. CORNEILLE: *Birds*, 1948, gouache on paper.

92. CORNEILLE: *Le port en tête*, watercolour, ink, collage and newsprint on paper.

93. CORNEILLE: *Le retour du marin*, 1949, oil on canvas.

94. CORNEILLE: *Le rythme joyeux de la ville*, 1949, oil on canvas.

95. CORNEILLE: *Village indigène*, 1951, oil on canvas.

96. CORNEILLE: *Fish*, 1950, watercolour on paper.

97. CORNEILLE: *Pierres et fleurs*, 1955, oil on canvas.

98. CORNEILLE: *Le port blanc* or *Heure matinale*, 1956, oil on canvas.

99. CORNEILLE: *Dans un jardin avec des oiseaux*, 1962, oil on canvas.

100. CORNEILLE: *Terre pastorale*, 1966, oil on canvas.

101. CORNEILLE: *Palmier-roi*, 1972, acrylic on canvas.

102. ROOSKENS: *Composition*, undated (ca. 1950), oil on canvas.

103. ROOSKENS: *Composition*, 1952, oil on canvas.

104. ROOSKENS: *African Forms*, 1954, oil on canvas.

105. ROOSKENS: *Woman with Bird*, 1968, oil on canvas.

106. WOLVECAMP: *Explosion*, 1948, oil on canvas.

107. NIEUWENHUYS: *Sleepwalking Rooster*, ca. 1949, oil, cardboard, collage on canvas.

108. WOLVECAMP: *Composition B3*, 1949, oil on canvas.

109. WOLVECAMP: *Tauromachie*, 1957, oil on canvas.

110. BRANDS: *Two Shapes*, 1949, oil on canvas.

111. BRANDS: *The Watchmaker's Wife*, 1952, oil on canvas.

112. BRANDS: *The Black Tower* or *Activité magique*, 1951, oil on canvas.

113. BRANDS: *Small Black Moon*, 1949, waste material on wood.

114. BRANDS: *Dynamic Landscape*, 1976, oil on canvas.

115. LUCEBERT: *Orpheus and the Animals*, 1952, gouache, ink and coloured pencils on paper.

116. LUCEBERT: *The Teeth of the Evidence*, 1952, gouache and collage on paper.

117. LUCEBERT: *Spanish Dance*, 1961, oil on canvas.

118. LUCEBERT: *Two Heads*, 1962, oil on canvas.

119. LUCEBERT: *The Prisoner*, 1964, oil on canvas.

120. VAN DER GAAG: *The Waiting*, 1951, terracotta.

121. TAJIRI: *One-day Sculptures on the Seine*, 1952, scrap metal.

122. ALECHINSKY: *Exercice de nuit*, 1950, gouache on paper.

123. ALECHINSKY: Three of a series of nine etchings entitled *Les Métiers*, 1948. a. *Le bûcheron*; b. *Le soldat*; c. *Le coiffeur*.

124. ALECHINSKY: *Les mers intérieurs*, 1958, oil on canvas.

125. ALECHINSKY: *Les polyglottes*, 1960, Indian ink and tempera on paper, glued on wood and finished with resin.

126. ALECHINSKY: *Alice grandit*, 1961, oil on canvas.

127. ALECHINSKY: *Dragon terrassant le petit Michel*, 1962, watercolour on paper, glued on canvas and finished with resin.

128. ALECHINSKY: *La jeune fille et la Mort*, 1967, acrylic and Indian ink on paper, glued on canvas.

129. ALECHINSKY: *L'Absent entouré*, 1973, acrylic on paper, glued on canvas.

130. ALECHINSKY: *The Franciscan Nun*, 1973, acrylic on paper, glued on canvas.

131. DOTREMONT: *"si désolé que soit...."*, 1974, Indian ink on paper.

132. DOTREMONT: *poudreux patatras de printemps*, 1969, Indian ink on paper.

133. DOTREMONT (text) & BALLE (painting): *Une peinture doit être ouverte et un peu fermée*, 1962, oil on canvas.

134. COX: *"Ne fait pas le vilain...."*, 1950, lithograph.

135. CLAUS: *Delfstof*, 1950, illustrated poem.

136. DOTREMONT (calligraphy) & ALECHINSKY (painting): *"Ondes extrêmes du feu...."*, 1974-79, Indian ink and acrylic on paper, glued on canvas.

137. REINHOUD: *Alien*, 1958, copper.

138. REINHOUD: *Les baladins*, 1972, copper.

139. ATLAN: *Samba zapotèque*, 1957, oil on canvas.

140. ATLAN: *Untitled*, ca. 1947, oil on canvas.

141. DOUCET: *Untitled*, 1949, watercolour on paper.

142. DOUCET: *Le dialogue de l'Egée*, 1978-81, oil on canvas.

143. GILBERT: *Mariposa*, 1948, oil on canvas.

144. GEAR: *Celtic Composition*, 1948, oil on canvas.

145. GÖTZ: *Nightmare*, 1948, monotype.

146. HULTÉN: *City Woman Kissing*, 1951, oil on canvas.

147. ÖSTERLIN: *Imaginary Red*, 1950, oil on canvas.

148. SVANBERG: *Imagination*, 1949, wax, tempera and ink on paper.

PHOTOCREDITS

The author and publisher would like to thank the following artists, museums, galleries, printers, publishers and private collectors for permission to use their reproduction material:

Pierre Alechinsky, Bougival, France; Galerie Ariel, Paris; De Bezige Bij, Amsterdam; Constant Nieuwenhuys, Amsterdam; Corneille, Paris; Duoprint BV, Hengelo, Netherlands; Fratelli Fabbri, Milan, Italy; Lotti van der Gaag, Paris; Karl Otto Götz, Germany; Edouard Jaguer, Paris; Sam and Ruth Kaner, Courtgallery, Copenhagen; Kunstverein, Hamburg; Lefèbre Gallery, New York; Galerie Nova Spectra, The Hague, Netherlands; M. and Mme. J. P. Paquot, Belgium; Reinhoud d'Haese, France; Smeets, Weert, Netherlands; Van Spijk, Venlo, Netherlands; Stedelijk Museum, Schiedam, Netherlands; J. Karel P. van Stuijvenberg, Caracas; Shinkichi Tajiri, Baarloo, Netherlands; Evert van Tright, Middelrode, Netherlands; Galerie Van de Loo, Munich; and Museum De Zonnehof, Amersfoort, Netherlands.

Photographs from other sources are gratefully acknowledged below:

Henk Brandsen, Amsterdam: figs. 64, 72; pp 9 (below), 15.
Carl-Henning Pedersens og Else Alfelts Museum, Herning, Denmark: figs. 30, 31, 37, 58, 59.
Ediciones Polígrafa, Barcelona: figs. 6, 11.
Gemeente Museum, The Hague, Netherlands: fig. 88.
Tom Haartsen, Schiedam, Netherlands: figs. 92, 96, 97, 98, 102, 103, 107, 110.
Museum van Hedendaagse Kunst, Ghent, Belgium: fig. 77.
Ron Huiskamp, Zwolle, Netherlands: fig. 109.
Henri Kessels: fig. 138.
Konstmuseet, Malmö, Sweden: figs. 146, 147, 148.
Louisiana Museum, Humlebaek, Denmark: fig. 36.
Rob Meijer, Leiden, Netherlands: fig. 114.
André Morain, Paris: figs. 123 (a, b, c), 136, 137.
Michel N'Guyen (copyright Galerie Maeght Lelong), Paris: fig. 126.
Nordjyllands Kunstmuseum, Aalborg, Denmark: figs. 42, 46, 55, 66.
Roald Pay, Copenhagen: figs. 51, 54.
Thijs Quispel, Oosthuizen, Netherlands: fig. 113.
Henny Riemens, Paris: fig. 9; p 21.
Jos de Ruijssenaars, Hooglanderveen, Netherlands: figs. 10, 133.
Rijksdienst Beeldende Kunst, The Hague, Netherlands: fig. 83.
Silkeborg Museum (Lars Bay), Silkeborg, Denmark: figs. 18, 22, 24, 25, 26, 40, 60.
Statens Museum for Kunst, Copenhagen (Hens Pedersen): figs. 19, 43, 47, 57.
Stedelijk Museum, Amsterdam: figs. 75, 78, 79, 85, 86, 89, 90, 100, 106, 108; pp 6, 11, 13 (left), 16 (b).
Stedelijk Van Abbe Museum, Eindhoven Netherlands: figs. 23, 84.
Archive Willemijn Stokvis, Amsterdam: figs. 1 (a, b, c, d), 3 (a, b, c, d), 8, 34, 35, 93, 111; pp 9 (above), 10 (left, middle), 12, 13 (left), 14, 16 (a, c, d, e, f), 15, 18, 19, 22, 24 (right), 26 (left), 27.
Tate Gallery, London: fig. 20.
Sabine Weiss, Paris: fig. 121; p 24 (left).